GET YOUR BUTT OUT THE DOOR

A 365-Day Motivational Runner's Companion

RANDY STEP

Published by Pacelli Publishing
Bellevue, Washington

Get Your Butt Out the Door: A 365-Day Motivational Runner's Companion

Cover and interior designed by Pacelli Publishing
Cover photo: Dr. Kathleen Step
Author photo: John Swanson

IRONMAN® VINEMAN® and 70.3®, and their respective logos, are registered trademarks of World Triathlon corporation in the United States and other countries. This independent publication has not been authorized, endorsed, sponsored or licensed by, nor has content been reviewed or otherwise approved by, World Triathlon Corporation dba IRONMAN.

Published by Pacelli Publishing
9905 Lake Washington Blvd. NE, #D-103
Bellevue, Washington 98004

Printed in the United States of America

ISBN 10: 1-933750-01-4
ISBN 13: 978-1-933750-01-9

Table of Contents

Dedication

To all the volunteers who make running events possible, helping us to reach our goals and live out our dreams. I am continually humbled by your spirit and generosity.

Praise for *Get Your Butt Out the Door*

"Randy writes in a way I relate to. The short thoughts that Randy makes concisely and effectively are perfect for a bump in encouragement." --*Gary*

"This might be my favorite book ever. I'm often way behind in my training, but you have inspired me to stay the course, even if I'm not as far along the course as I was hoping. I don't think I would still be running if it weren't for your writing. Seriously. It's motivated me through some tough times and trials and encouraged me through your own trials that you've shared to stay on my doctor to let me run! I thank you from the bottom of my heart and soles!" --*Allyssa*

"Love the Winter posts. It's so true, this is the time to get out and run as people head indoors from the cold weather. I have had some memorable, snow crunching runs. And yes, we can dress for the cold but the hot is harder to tame." --*Tamara*

"I want to tell you how impressed I am with your writing. I don't' head out without reading a page first, because they are eloquent. You are able to perfectly express in words the thoughts and feelings I have as a runner--one who loves it (although I'm not particularly skilled and am currently on the sidelines with an injury, ha)." --*Connie*

"I view running just as you do--a way of life, a meaningful pursuit amidst such frustrating, unjust politics--it's just great to hear some like minds out there. Thanks for all you do, and your words of wisdom!!" --*Sarah*

"Randy, you do an amazing job at making seemingly lofty goals seem real . . . so real that many new runners meet those goals and then surpass them. You guide, poke, and encourage a healthy happy lifestyle while giving us runners a place to gather. Be it to lick our wounds, praise each other in accomplishments or to gather our forces and pray for our injured friends. Thank you for all that you do and provide to us. May each of us have faith and never ever give up!" *--Dawn*

"I just wanted to thank you for the daily pokes. They are refreshing, timely, funny and keep me motivated to run. I enjoy them all and appreciate the encouraging themes. You effectively walk the line between motivation and information. Run forever." *--Joe*

"I am an avid runner and just wanted to take a minute to tell you how much I appreciate all you do. You are an amazing writer and a fantastic motivator!!! My husband and I love all that you do for running and for us crazy runners/athletes. Keep the positive vibes coming--I look forward to each one. Take care." *-- Tanya*

"I greatly enjoy reading your thoughts and perspectives on running, training, gear, and life in general. You continually reveal a new idea or point of view that I had not previously known about or heard of. I really appreciated your pages on Winter and the power of positive thinking. I repeat the same mantra to myself too. And it does actually help. I love Winter . . . I love Winter . . . I love Winter." *--Kellie*

"Each page is heartfelt and sincere--I think you captured what many of us are thinking and feeling about getting out

that door. THANK YOU for continuing to inspire us all." --
Susan

Introduction

How often do we really want to head out for a run? For most of us, I'd guess 20 percent of the time. How often are we happy we got the run in? One hundred percent of the time. So, knowing this, why is it so hard to get our butts out that door? As they say, it seems to take every trick in the book to make the daily run happen. Well, this is that book. It is not a book meant to be read from cover to cover, but to be a go-to before heading out, especially if you are waffling or making excuses for missing the run.

Okay, these daily entries are not really tricks, more like insights into our simple but amazing sport, hopefully offering a deeper understanding of all that the run gives us. You run, you get it, perhaps you get it as well as the author. Regardless, each daily entry may provide a poke, a push, a pang of guilt, whatever, but always a reminder that you are a runner and today's run will affirm your way of life. On second thought, they are tricks, and it is now your book, so if you want to read it straight through, that's okay too.

January

January 1 - Blame Caesar

When Caesar created the Julian calendar, he thought it would be appropriate for January, Janus' namesake month, to be the doorway to a new year. As for New Year's resolutions, January was just a bad choice. Perhaps if Julius lived in the North, the year would start in Spring, and it would make sense. We could work to change this, but I am guessing it would be more difficult than getting people to call the half-marathon a Pikermi. (Look it up) That said, it is time to plan the year, ease into training and get on a roll. I stress "ease into training" because too much too soon is the norm for fitness resolutions, leading to pain and failure. A rule of thumb: don't increase any activity more than 10 percent per week. For example, run 10 miles one week and up it to 11 the next. The rule of thumb means upping your running more than 10 percent will inflict as much pain as if you were beating yourself with a stick larger than the width of your thumb. More on Caesar later.

currere et adepto – Get out and run!

January 2 - Everything to excess!

I ended the year by snowshoeing with reckless abandon on double Black Diamonds and getting in a long hilly road run that included some black ice patches. Then, late into New Year's Eve, one bad dance move cost me big time, and today I'm limping and on the side lines. A lesson in all this? Avoid the dangerous stuff, ha! If you are starting off the year healthy, remember, running is the priority, do not let ego get in the way, make smart choices and come Spring, your running will rock!

There are a lot of choices on what to do today, choose to run some miles!

January 3 - Fat to 50 miles

The resolutions are in full swing and as you know, I am a fan! My son-in-law has certainly jumped right past the couch to 5K program and signed up for the 50-Mile Ultra at Run Woodstock. He calls his goal "from fat to 50 miles." I love it! Yes, joining a family like mine that has gone ALL IN on the running gig was sure to have influenced his plan and commitment. I believe many of us would benefit from committing to a goal that would turn our so called "normal life" on its head. Consider signing up to run farther than you could possibly imagine. Only after you commit and start your journey will you find that your self-imposed limits were nonsense and that you are utterly amazing.

Get out the door and start your personal journey today. Go all in!

January 4 - Keep a log

Yes, fitness tracking apps can help get your butt out the door. That said, there is still some magic in writing it down and seeing it each day. Simple numbers, totals and streaks can be tremendous motivation, and a log increases your chance of success. Consider this scenario, with and without a log: you promised yourself to get in a run sometime today, but family situations kept getting in your way. It is a dark, rainy Sunday night, and you can finally go for the run, but you are tired and the depressing weather has you thinking about the couch. Getting out the door tonight will not be easy; then you look over your running log and start to admire your streak of consistency. You have run at least 3 days each week for the past 19 weeks and have run at least 20 miles each week. A run tonight will make it 20 weeks straight, a personal record--and you also notice that you need at least 3 miles tonight to hit 20 for the week, another personal record streak! When you get home you can record two records in your log. Without the log, would you have run?

The log makes a great diary, log some miles in one-- TODAY!

January 5 - January does not totally suck

Yes, January weather can suck, but January also gives us the clean-slate feel of the running year ahead. January--a great time to plan, to dream and to start. Making plans and resolutions in a Winter month is a valuable catalyst to get us out the door when we need it most. If you've received some holiday running gifts; these also can help light the fire in January. If not, go buy yourself some; most likely they are on sale! Call it an investment in motivation, one sure to beat the market. A great resolution is to get online and enter a Spring race. Knowing you have committed to an upcoming event will push you out of a warm bed and out the door so your resolution will be safe.

Go log some precious early, clean-slate, January miles!

January 6 - You look marvelous, or soon will

The look of the distance runner is long, lean, and defined. A look of balance, action, and endurance, not a body built in a gym, but on the roads and trails, sculpted in the natural environment by simple hard work, one foot in front of the other. The skin of a runner has an outdoor look. Wind, sun and sweat have given it texture, color, and wear. An alive and real look, unlike skin that lives under incandescent light alone, not to mention tan lines that tell a story of how this body spends its time in motion, in nature. Natural beauty, beauty by natural means. The runner's body is not the result of a 30-day miracle training program but one that evolved from consistency and passion for the sport.

Get outside, get the look.

January 7 - Be prepared . . . to run!

On the Winter run here in Michigan, it is not unusual for the temperature to start off at 20 degrees, go up to a sunny 40, then get cloudy, windy and down to 15, all in the same hour. Yikes! A lightweight, great-fitting running backpack can be your thermostat, allowing you to take stuff off, stash it, and pull it back out when needed. Having extra dry clothes in Winter can give you a sense of security, especially if something happens and you must stop or walk. Pack like a Boy Scout; include your phone, toilet tissue, gels or sport bars, water, cash, snow traction devices and whatever else will give you the confidence to head out the door!

You are a self-sufficient athlete off on an adventure. Oh yeah!

January 8 - Sanity maintenance

Winter is a time to make sure we just get out the door consistently. The runs do not have to be hard or long, but basic maintenance for the body and sanity. Any Winter races we enter can be fun, social events where we do not stress over pace or time. Winter can give us time to learn about our sport, write a training plan for ourselves and set some goals. Make this your year to run or set a personal best in a half-marathon, marathon, or triathlon. Daunting goals, but not when you have a plan in place and set yourself up for success.

Study and plan, but do not miss today's run!

January 9 - Sneak in a couple more

I always say, run smart but do not let the weather get in the way of your run. Dress for it and adjust the distance or course to make it safe so you can still get out there. That said, when the weather, the schedule, or anything that makes the run go well is in your favor, sneak in some extra miles. Not only will you be adding some miles to the log, miles you might have lost to bad days, but a bit of longer run, especially in Winter, does wonders for your mood and self-esteem. The power of a good run can leave you with a smile that lingers for days!

When the going is good, keep going! Then again, when going through hell do the same!

January 10 - Winter runs make us bullet proof

Outdoor Winter running will give you strength and balance. The heavy clothing and varied footing get the ancillary muscles of the body into play. When on the roads and in the woods, you will be seeing amazing natural stuff you won't on a treadmill! Yes, treadmill running is way better than no running and has its own unique benefits, but you do need to get outside consistently for sanity and all the above.

Run against the wind, then with it!

January 11 - You are a running role model

As role models, we have a responsibility to not only run safe but to show respect for others and the environment we enjoy. When we see runners not yielding to other pedestrians as if they are on some important mission, we cringe. The same goes for runners wearing dark clothing and running with, instead of against traffic, creating unsafe situations for themselves and others. When we drive past a runner in the dark wearing a reflective vest we should call out and thank them for it. The list goes on, from common sense headphone use to urinating in public, we need to use good judgement and elevate the sport we love.

Get out there and make us proud.

January 12 - A year-long plan keeps us motivated

If you have not already, make a plan for your mileage buildup that takes aim at a longer Spring race that includes some races leading up to the ultimate goal. With a plan, your chance of success goes up big-time. After that key event, plan an easy couple of weeks, then a buildup of running miles with your sights set on a Fall goal. The truth is, you can't have hard days without easy days, and you can't have a peak season without an off-season, and without a plan you have no season. Make a plan, your results along the way will keep your fire lit.

Look at the big picture, plan, then look at the door, open it and run.

January 13 - Champions are made in Winter

These wicked runs will give us the armor we need to fight our way back to the higher mileage runs as the world thaws. The mental toughness needed to get out into the cold will give us the confidence to survive anything the Spring long runs and races throw our way. Bring it on! No matter how tough it gets out there, we will be tougher!

Let's run in this crap!

January 14 - Isn't all that running going to ruin your joints?

I hate dumb questions, but it is part of life. I have been running 5 to 7 days a week for 40-something years, and my joints are just fine, thanks. Google, "Is running bad for your knees?" The info will make you smile, and you will want to get out the door. Stuff like: epidemiological studies of long-term runners show that they generally are less likely to develop osteoarthritis in the knees than people of the same age who do not run and some scientists have speculated that running may protect knees because it also often is associated with relatively low body mass, and carrying less weight is known to reduce the risk for knee arthritis. So there!

Get out and run those knees into shape!

January 15 - Still diggin' the run

I must admit, with more than 40 years of getting out the door, I am about as obsessed with running as I've ever been, wallowing in it like a pig in mud. My running has taken me around the world and around the block. Another new year and it is time for new plans to keep the fire lit. I am committed to run the 50K Trail Weekend, several half-marathons and the Travers City 70.3 . . . so far! I hope you have caught the running curse and stay over on the dark side with me till the end. If not, today is a great day to enter a couple of long races to get the fire burning.

Run or grow old and moldy.

January 16 - I repeat the important stuff

Running is personal. Our goals, our pace, our motivation and our satisfaction all come from our perception of our running and in this case, perception is our reality. I find it cool that what we put into our running and what we take from it is pretty much the same as the fastest runner to the slowest runner in the world. Sure, we can't help comparing ourselves to others, but the reality is that how others run is pretty much irrelevant; their run is their run and our run is ours. Each and every time we run out the door, whether we run with a friend or line up with thousands of others at an event, whether the run goes well or is pure torture, our run becomes a part of who we are, something that can't be taken away or compared.

Collect some miles today; they will be with you forever.

January 17 - Get out and jog in your tennis shoes, or perhaps just do a half-jog

I'm sure you have a list of stuff that drives you nuts, mine includes: (1) people who call running shoes "tennis shoes" (Heck, running shoes are perhaps the worst shoes you could wear playing tennis!), (2) the term "jogger," (3) people who refer to any running event as a marathon (Do they really not know a marathon is 26.2 miles?) and (4) the term that bothers me the most, "half-marathon." It is a 13.1-mile race, and everywhere outside the U.S. it is called 21K. Yes, the full marathon happens to be 42K but we don't call a 5K, half of a 10K, it makes no sense to use the word half, these races are specific distances we race, they are not half of anything! Venting does make one feel better!

Get out and run hard to clear your head of stuff that pisses you off!

January 18 - A day off, or a 2-mile run?

To some people, a 2-mile run doesn't seem worth the effort. Is it worth it to dress, run and shower all for less than a half hour of running? My answer is, "You bet!" The two-mile run is highly underrated. Two miles offer a microcosm of all that I love about the sport. It is mentally easy for me to get out the door knowing I only have 2 miles to run. I take the first half-mile slowly, after breaking a sweat I stop to stretch a bit. The next mile I run at a good hard effort, about 10K pace, and the final half-mile is a cool down. I run home, shoulders relaxed and at a comfortable pace. I have finished a run and feel fresh, awake, and alive, like a day off, only better. I have not had to put a zero in my log! Tired of taking days off each week? Run 2!

You are not a wimp; most people can't run one mile!

January 19 - We live here, we run here

Whatever the weather, we can handle it. Heck, we choose to live where we do for a reason. The adventure of weather adds variety and excitement to our daily runs, walks or slogs. You bring it on, we go play in it! The satisfaction of just getting out, breaking a healthy sweat and breathing in the fresh air is what we live for. Hot, cold, windy, wet, we have not found anything that can stop us yet.

Enjoy it, now!

January 20 - Do your running homework

There are only a couple more weeks of what I call off-season running, then . . . no more mister nice guy! In January we make our Spring race plans, in February, we ramp up the mileage a bit to halt the Winter pounds. Your homework is to write a training schedule to prepare you for a long Spring race. The schedule will be your coach and will always be there telling you when you miss a day! Find a schedule that you believe in and use it as a base. Tweak it to your real-life schedule and mileage and it will be a key part of your get-out-the-door arsenal.

Did you do your homework? Did you run today?

January 21 - Some days, we deserve a finisher's medal

This busy life has enough obstacles keeping us from the run, let alone having tough weather to wear down our resolve. One cold weather solution is to not overthink it, just overdress and run out the door. Once out and running, you can then consider the distance, the weather and if you should circle back and shed some clothes. If the wind is wicked, look to find a stretch that is protected, then perhaps repeat it for a while, maybe for the entire run. Make it a point to notice something different on each lap--birds, types of trees, or how your footprints are adding up in the snow. You could find yourself getting more into it on each lap and heading home only because your window of time is up. Okay, maybe I am getting down to the bottom of my bag of our get-out-the-door tricks, but we will prevail!

Run out the door first, then give it some thought.

January 22 - Choose to run

Every day we have hard choices to make, for example: (1) More time in a warm bed in the morning or wake to an alarm and run out into the cold and dark. (2) Get home from work, grab a cold beverage and snack food then hit the couch for some tube, or lace up the shoes and drag our tired, end-of-the-day feeling body out the door for some miles. These really are hard choices.

Fortunately, we have become runners and have learned through hard work and making the hard choices that once we are out the door we will get into the rhythm of the run. Once out the door, our bodies will become warm, fluid and energized, our head will clear and the stress of the day will roll off and leave us feeling free, alive, and clean. We will finish with our self-esteem and confidence raised, ready to take on the day or evening in a way no sedentary person can possibly understand. Share the gift, drag a friend out of bed for a run--perhaps send them this book!

Make the hard choice, run!

January 23 – I love Winter running, yep, I love Winter running

The chill in the morning air and the crunch of the snow underfoot; it gets no better. Sure, love and hate are choices, and because Winter is part of living in Michigan, my wife and I made a decision to say we love Winter rather than complain about it. To help make this happen, whenever the topic of Winter comes up, we answer with our new mantra: We love Winter, We love Winter, WE LOVE WINTER. The truth--we were not always big fans of most aspects of Winter, but by dressing properly and getting out for the daily run, we find we actually do love the active outdoor times and with our new attitude and our new mantra we continue to find more and more to love about Winter. Join us and make the "I love Winter" choice!

We love Winter running, so we will run today!

January 24 - Don't miss today

As we make plans for tomorrow and worry about the future, we rob ourselves of today. The worry is a waste. What we do today and the way we live today will set us up for tomorrow. Trust your instincts to live, love and learn today the way you want to every day going forward and it becomes what you do. Tomorrow, you will live for tomorrow and it will be even better than today. For example, head out the door to enjoy the adventure of today's Winter run. Yes, it's cold, windy, gray and the footing is awful, but you know you will be immediately rewarded for your effort. Just by getting outside your man-made confines and enjoying the natural wonders of nature you will feel in command of your environment. You will be building strength by using muscles needed to control yourself in the snow and this will make you a more powerful and versatile runner tomorrow. You will also be increasing your capacity for endurance and are training for an even more exceptional run tomorrow. You will be ready to race and be able to run longer and faster, not by planning but by living and doing!

Live, run, and more will come.

January 25 - When is your run scheduled tomorrow?

When the weather, the economy or something else out of your control has you down, it is time for a head-clearing run, a run with more value than ever for your mental and physical sanity. Unfortunately, the motivation to get out the door for such a run drops inversely to the misery index, which is a dilemma. I remind you of this because knowing your demons puts you in a better position to fight them. Life is too busy to find time to get in a run, and depressing news continues to come along, so make sure the run is scheduled in advance. When the reminder alarm goes off and it says it is time to run, you will be successful in making it a priority. Ding! Now get out that door!

When it is on the calendar, nothing can stop you!

January 26 - January is a great time for CORE, CORE, CORE!

As an obsessed runner, my goal is to run for a lifetime, and for that to happen, the body needs core strength, recovery, and seasonal changes in training to hold together. Of course, what I'd like to do is just go out and run long. Dang, nothing good comes easily, but, like so many things in life, the sacrifices needed to accomplish long-term goals are worth it. I consider December and January as off-season running months, a time where distance and speed are ignored and our running satisfaction can be taken from nothing more than constancy--just getting out the door. With the cutback in running, we have time for planks, other core work, strength, and balance, with perhaps yoga or Pilates. I like simple workouts where you use the weight of your body. Once Winter starts to break and our mileage goes up, we will have the strength to handle the increased stress.

I suggest you close your office door now, and sneak in some one-legged squats!

January 27 - Running is illogical

As Spock would say about running, it is illogical. The sweat, pain and the energy used to get from point A to point A or B may seem pointless, perhaps even wasteful to someone without deeper knowledge about what the runner is experiencing. In ways, running has aspects similar to art, music, and religion. Without personally experiencing what we experience, even a well-delivered explanation would fall short. For these reasons, many of us were forced to run for the first time, or perhaps tricked into it. However it happened, we obviously glimpsed something hiding below the surface, something that made us run again, and again, and again, with each run adding to the richness of what the run gives back.

Get out and defy logic.

January 28 - I admit I'm cheating Winter a bit

I jumped in my car to get to a place to run out of the wind and cold . . . and 18 hours later I ended up in Florida. Watching the temperature on the dash work its way from -7 to 80 degrees was highly motivational and kept me going. A few audio books helped make the drive less painful. I have been enjoying tropical trail runs this week and will sneak in a half-marathon this weekend before heading back on Monday. If at all possible, punch a hole in Winter with a warm escape, just another tool to get us through. Next weekend, I'll be road tripping up to Traverse City, Michigan for the Bigfoot 5K and 10K snowshoe race. Life it too short not to throw in a spur of the moment road trip, North or South.

Do something spontaneous, this is not dress rehearsal.

January 29 - Time for recess!

We joke about the child inside us that appears in our actions from time to time. I believe that, in reality, as a child we know our most important needs and they do not change much as we age. These needs include playtime--the joyful and learning time of our day, which is a time for fitness and self-discovery. Somehow, as we grow and face new responsibilities as adults, society makes "play" out to be a guilty pleasure and not the essential part of the day that it really is.

Put on your play clothes and get out the door!

January 30 – Every day can be New Year's Day

Just because another year has started, don't let your head trick you into the idea that because you missed making some positive changes to your life by a few days it's too late to do so. Every day of the year is a good day to set goals and commit to positive changes, and if you falter along the way, every day is a good day to start over and re-commit yourself! Nothing good comes easy. Never ever give up hope; the rewards along the way will be worth all the effort. Resolutions can change your life. Make them, and believe.

Start your year today with a run, of course!

January 31 - Getting fit is time well spent

The great part about not being in shape is that a short workout is such an efficient use of time--a few miles and you are wasted, fulfilled. As you rack up the miles and your fitness level goes up, the time commitment to get that same wonderful wasted feeling gets serious. But there is a plus side--as the workout gets long, the satisfaction also goes up. So much like everything in our humble sport, it's all win, win.

Run 'til you're shot, it's worth it!

27

February

February 1 - Savor each day

Remember your mom trying to get you to eat every scrap on your plate by saying, "There are starving people in the world!" As if your eating will help someone from starving. But it could piss off a starving person to watch you waste food! So, if you are healthy and able to run and are blowing off the run for some lame reason, think about the injured runners out there who would do almost anything to be in your shoes! Okay, once again, as I think about it, your miles won't do a thing for someone who can't run, but it would piss me off to know you're not doing everything you can to get out that door!

Don't waste the run, or anything else.

February 2 - Everything we ever need to know, we can learn from our running

Long-term goal planning, delayed gratification, moderation, discipline, meditation, love of the natural world, increased self-esteem, soul-searching, being honest with ourselves, and the list goes on. Runners make the world a better place, for sure. If everyone ran, there would be no time for pettiness, war or hate and the healthcare crisis would fade away with each footfall. You may say I'm a dreamer, but I'm not the only one, maybe someday they will join us, and the world will run as one. Each step we run offers us the opportunity to be role models, each step gives us a chance to change the world for the better.

Don't just imagine it, get out the door, run, and make the world a better place.

February 3 - An ugly run

Last night, I got on the gear, slapped myself a few times (short on sleep) and headed out into an icy rain. Every step was an effort, I felt dead-legged and worked for every breath. Five minutes in I decided I would attempt to keep suffering for another 25 minutes after making such an effort to get out the door. After what I figured was 25 minutes later, I looked at my watch to find it had only been only been 10 minutes! I forced out the full 30 minutes, every one of them torture. The moral of the story? Some days just suck.

The good part, once I was finished, I felt just fine, I was glad I got in a run and I am happy that not all runs go this badly! I share this story with you so that you know that you are not alone out there on the ugly days.

Slog on, I'm with you!

February 4 - Even runners get the flu

My weekly goal is to motivate us out the door, but the goal also includes keeping us healthy, so we miss as few days as possible. As runners, we get a ton of physical and mental health benefits from our lifestyle. Unfortunately, susceptibility to the flu is not one of our run's benefits, dang. I have several friends fighting the flu currently and I sure do not want to join them. We runners need to take the same precautions as the rest of the world including hand-washing and getting the flu shot. Yes, get out the door for your run, but this time of the year, take recovery days after hard or long workouts and be additionally cautious around crowds or anyone who might be contagious. Due to a hard run, our immune system will be a bit compromised until we recover, so, no kissing strangers after long runs until after May 1st!

Run, rest, wash your hands and we can hug again in the Spring.

February 5 - The running time machine

Last night I put in some miles on the streets where my running passion first bloomed. It was the 35th anniversary of the Redford Road Runners Club. I headed out with many members of the same crew I ran with 35 years before. Admittedly, we looked like caricatures of those young, fast, punks of old, but as the pace quickened and the breakaway groups formed, the same old running magic was there. I jumped into a pack I thought I could hang with and as we put the hammer down and got into a groove I was transported to the time before wrinkles. For sure I was working as hard as I did back then, perhaps at a pace a few minutes per mile slower, but unless I looked at a watch or into a mirror, nothing had changed. Dig it.

Run today, so you can run forever.

February 6 - Run proud

I saw a Facebook post with a picture of a 13.1 sticker on a car, the comment was, I don't give a sh-t. I was thinking to respond with, "Well I do!" Seriously, I smile when I know I'm around a kindred soul, someone who understands my running world, a small sticker tells a big story. A story of dedication, determination, a story about a goal oriented individual, a positive role model. I find it a refreshing sticker, not politics, religion, or a controversial subject . . . or so I thought!

Run proud and loud, and put on a sticker to prove it!

February 7 - Today's run will prepare you for anything

As runners, we all have setbacks, it is part of our sport. Setbacks can vary in severity and the road back to the front of the pack can be a long one, but it is what we do. It is what we've trained to do and what makes this competitive running life so precious that it is perhaps the essence of our lives. The goal is always clear, to get back to the starting line . . . and to share what we have learned to help others get to get to the starting line. Every moment of this life is precious--even moments like when my friend Amy was hit by a truck that broke half the bones in her body and put her in a coma. It was a setback that running prepared her for. Three years later, she is back on the starting line.

Live, love, learn and run, so when the time comes, you will know you will run again.

February 8 - We are works in progress

It is hard not to notice when we stare in amazement at a world class distance athlete's body--the chiseled look of speed, endurance and movement, even while standing still. Not a body built in a gym but one with defined muscles sculpted by long miles and hard work. The distance athlete has an uneven tan, tight skin and an outdoor look of challenge and adventure. We may have different genetics and life history than the Olympians, but we are all athletes working on being the best we can.

Let's get out the door and chisel away to our own level of greatness!

February 9 - Bad weather = Good runs

Bring it on: the worse the weather, the more valuable the run, both physically and mentally. There is something about a cold dark morning run in horrid conditions that gives a feeling of power, what I call a Rambo Run. It's like you have something over everyone else. These runs can make us feel like superheroes, something a run on a beautiful day just cannot match. Get out there and feel the power!

If it sucks out, run, and feel the power!

February 10 - Find a training partner

Knowing some poor soul is out there waiting for you at 6 a.m. will force you out of bed and out the door. The guilt associated with blowing off a run date is strong motivation. Where to find a partner that runs your pace and fits into your schedule? It is tricky and you might have to make some sacrifices to make it work but it will be worth it. Go to running clubs, running stores, weekly runs, or even local races. Strike up conversations with those around you at your pace. Get to the important question, where do you live? Running partners are not easy to find but the right one can challenge you, keep you consistent and add to your running experience like nothing else.

They need you too, run out and find them!

February 11 - Runners make nerds look like the prom kings and queens!

We fart, we burp, we pee in the woods, we change in our car, we have piles of clothes that stink, and we have more shoes than Lady GaGa. We actually pay big bucks to run 3.1 miles and have an embarrassing large pile of tee shirts to prove we did this. In this modern, temperature-controlled world we are often, wet and cold or hot and sweaty. We have big ugly plastic watches that cost as much as a Rolex. All that said, how come I have this smug feeling of satisfaction and superiority over the average American every time I run out that door?

We know why. Smile and get out there!

February 12 - Run, but run smart

I sure like it better when I get to talk smack, when my body is clicking along like an indestructible running machine. Then there are days like today, where I do the toughest thing there is in our sport, something smart that feels embarrassing. I cut the run short because of some darn pain behind my knee, perhaps a bit of the old IT band. Worse yet, I'm running with a couple of other runners who I talked into running a snowy trail in the dark and I leave them to return to my car, pack some snow on the leg, and head home. We all need to be put in our place and the body has a way of doing it better than anyone can. Ice and a few easy days and I will be back out on the trail. This would not have been the case in the early run years; my ego and I would have hammered ourselves into a month off.

Run, but run smart, yes, I repeated that.

February 13 - Let Winter know how you really feel – From my daughter Anna

Let's face it, people, this Winter is never going to end! I'm cold, I'm tired, and I do not want to get my butt out the door! I'm tired of washing my running jackets, I'm tired of hunting for the perfect hat for the specific temperature of the day, I'm tired of wet socks. So, you know what Winter, SUCK IT!

Let me explain to you what I just did there. When I was a high school runner I invented a little game called "1, 2, 3, complain." The concept was very simple--on those days I just didn't want to do it, I would say "1, 2, 3, COMPLAIN" and spend the first minute or so of my run complaining out loud. So put your shoes on and get your butt out the door, start your run by shouting about all the things you're sick of, maybe even throw in a SUCK IT, WINTER! It will get you giggling, you'll have gotten all that nonsense off your chest and you're already through the hardest few minutes of your run.

Dig all your Winter gear out and get out the door

February 14 - Motivation is a choice

Motivation is a feeling, and feelings are a choice, like so many things in life. For example, happiness is a choice. You can sit in a rush hour traffic jam and pound on the steering wheel, or you can appreciate the time alone with your thoughts and sort out the world. You can bitch, moan and make excuses not to run when the weather gets cold and windy, or you can run out the door and thumb your nose to the weather, laugh at it, and show your neighbors you really are a nut. So, when your mind seems to be made up that it wants to do anything but run, go run. Tell your head to "get with the program or be miserable, it's up to you, I'm running!" Feel bad, rundown, unmotivated, good! Once this run is finished you will have a much greater feeling of satisfaction and accomplishment than an easy run on a nice day. So, the next time you feel unmotivated. Get your lazy a-- out of bed and . . .

Go hammer!

February 15 - Think Spring

February--yes, it may still seem like the dead of Winter, but it's time for the start of more serious training. For those of us planning on a long Spring race, now is the time to start upping the mileage and running with purpose. In a few months, the Winter wimps will stand in awe as we step up to the line and speak with our feet! Actually, the wimps have been standing in awe of us all Winter each time they see us out there! The truth is, nobody cares about our run but us but if just the thought of someone caring gets us out the door, so be it!

I care, get out there and make it happen.

February 16 - Find running shoes that love you

Don't you just love it when you find running shoes that love you back! Currently, I'm having an affair with my Brooks Cascadia trail shoes; from fit to function. I can't find a negative thing about them. I'm not in the same groove with my road shoes right now and I think that's enforcing the love of the shoes that are working. Running is such a simple sport and our few pieces of equipment become quite special. And yes, new toys help get you out the door. Look for the joy in every aspect of our simple sport.

Let's get out and play with our toys!

February 17 - Rave runs come unexpectedly, be ready

My last run to qualify as a rave run was not where or how I would have expected it. On a snowy dark February evening I headed out to run 4 miles of half-mile loops around a nondescript industrial complex near my office before heading home, hoping to miss a messy rush hour. The loop is plowed, lit and has no traffic after 5 p.m. I was running loop after loop with a light snow falling, just me, my thoughts and the mantra of my footfalls. At some point I became fully conscious of the run like waking from a dream and marveled at the beauty of the snow, strange hallows around the lights and wild shadow movements created by my run as I moved forward. The unexpected beauty shocked me out of what I can only call meditation. I had planned for a boring 4 miles but realized time had slipped by me and I had run almost 6 joyful miles. I love this sport, it constantly amazes me.

Get out the door, today might be the one.

February 18 - Running, it's all good

I love the peaceful solitude of a training run alone, my time to sort out the tangled world. I also like to run with friends, sometimes for the conversation, where pace and distance matter little, and sometimes for the motivation, where pace and distance are maxed and challenged. Last but not least, I love to line up on race day and find out where I stand, mostly to compete with myself but yes, to see how my time compares to others and to duke it out! Running is a personal sport; nobody else really cares about our race times, our weekly mileage or our running pace. What a refreshing and wonderful running life we have, it really is all good.

This run's for you.

February 19 - Running, as extreme as sports get

Running gets us down to bedrock. Each run requires physical and mental strength just to head out the door. Some days, our body lets us know it really doesn't want to do this, much like pulling an unwilling dog on a leash with his paws kicking and dragging. Ah, but on some days our bodies are jumping and barking at the door, ready to go! We marvel at the "X" Games and sports that are called "extreme," when in reality, there is no more extreme sport than distance running, one that has us heading out day after day to do battle and keep the edge, regardless of how we feel or what the conditions, knowing that nothing good comes easy and what we will get for our hard work and extreme behavior is good, very good. When race day dawns, hang on to that leash tightly and be ready to keep up with a happy, well-trained body, pulling you forward to personal greatness. Now, give yourself a pat on the head!

Train and run like an animal!

February 20 - Lick your wounds

Winter is a good time to be nursing a running injury—NOT! It's never a good time, but better than the glorious days of Spring or Fall. So, injured or not, Winter is a good time for CORE, CORE, CORE, yoga, and all those other insufferable non-aerobic activities! Time for a deep breath--it could be worse. Sure, it's like saying, "Mrs. Lincoln, sorry about your loss but how did you enjoy the play?" For those of you gimping out there, grief shared is grief diminished, I hope this cheered you up!

Enjoy every healthy day, and the broken days as best you can.

February 21 - It's never easy

I planned on a midday run but as I looked out my office window at the gray, windy, cold rainy day, I was losing interest. Knowing it would be my only chance to run, I reluctantly pulled on my stuff and headed out. What a waste of negative thoughts and negative energy! One minute into my run I was warm, clicking along and loving this rainy adventure. You would think I'd know better after all these years, but tricking myself out the door seems to remain a constant in this running life, go figure.

It's always worth it, including today!

February 22 - Walk, run, race

The daily run, our daily bread, can seem like enough; the run's positive influence on our physical and mental state are unquestionable, so why race? A valid question. Heck, some people survive this world without running at all, but we know if they had found running, they may have had a more rich and fulfilling life. I believe it's the same with racing. Many runners put in the miles and never toe the line. Those of us who have entered, set goals and raced, realize that this wonderful sport has even more to offer. When we race, regardless of our condition or age, we line up and find out where we stand and attempt to better our performance--we become athletes. Mostly, we compete with ourselves, to see what we have in us, to be honest with ourselves, to run smart, to give our best on the given day. In our day-to-day family and work life we do so many things that giving our best is not so black and white. When we race, it's true, it's clear, it's real. We get down to bedrock, we give witness to the person we are and gather insight into who we might be. And yes, we run against those around us, giving us the momentum and excitement of knowing where we stand in the physical order of things. For us, not being last may be a more valuable and uplifting race experience than it was to the person who won. We get all this from toeing the line!

Train today so you can race tomorrow!

February 23 - How does that line go? All I really need to know I learned by running a marathon

I learned long-term goal planning, time management and what is meant by delayed gratification. I learned about my body, how to eat healthy and get enough rest. I learned anger management (in the late miles), how to deal with success and how to deal with failure. I learned who I was and who I could be. Yes, somewhat cliché, but running a marathon will change your life forever, I suggest you move it up on the bucket list if you haven't already. For those of you marathoners, another will refresh your success skills!

Today's miles will lead you there.

February 24 - Running and Passion

Without a fire in our heart, the world seems cold. I'm not completely sure of the meaning of life, but having a passion seems to be a piece of the puzzle. For those of us lucky enough to have found running and have made it our passion, we understand how important having a focus that drives us can be. We are fortunate that our passion is healthy and non-threatening to others. I also believe that those who have found a passion are much more understanding and accepting of others with passions, even those much different than ours. Passion gives us common ground--we can relate to those who are really into something.

Live it up out there and show and share your passion.

February 25 - You are impressive

The demographics of runners are pretty impressive. I guess that means I'm writing this to a smart, educated, self-directed, hard-working group that understands commitment. Hmm, that puts the pressure on me. You do what you do with little fanfare or recognition. That said, I'm proud of the running community and to be a part of it. We run side by side in races with a quiet but special bond, knowing exactly what it took to get where we are.

Be proud of your run today.

February 26 - Never let the weather affect your planned run

I am sure you can relate. I put off the Monday morning run at 20 degrees opting for the day-end run with a predicted high of 40. The morning was still, clear and the sunrise was beautiful. Instead, I ran that night in the dark, pouring rain and perhaps mid-30s with no chance of 40 in sight. Each footfall was a cold wet shock, you get the picture. The rule: Never let the weather affect your planned run. When race day dawns, you have no choice in the matter and you'd better be ready and know how to dress and run in all conditions. There are a ton of things that will come along to thwart the day's run; weather should never be one of them. If the rain had been in the morning, I should still have headed out. Didn't I just say that?

Get out and run in that crap!

February 27 - Yes, you can run there

Running to work is truly an environmentally friendly and rewarding experience with an added time management perk, especially if it lets you escape wasted time in morning traffic. The excuse is often that there is no shower at work. The answer is to shower and prepare for work before you head out on the run. Leave a set of work clothes at the office and any makeup or other prep items you need to look ready for the day. Because sweat is sterile and you just took a shower, as long as you run in clean running gear, there is no "smell" associated with your workout. Leave a clean towel at work to dry off the sweat. Even better, leave a set of this stuff at work all the time to give you even more flexibility. And yes, you can put on the dirty stuff to run home in! Don't live close enough? No excuse! Find a Park & Ride lot that is running distance from work, and run from there.

Enjoy the morning "rush."

February 28/29 - Run guilt free

Do you ever find yourself sneaking away from work, friends or family to get in a run? Or not mentioning it or letting anyone see you come and go because they may question your sense of priority? The truth is, there is so much we get from the run that it can't always be explained or appreciated by the non-runner. That said, If we get caught, but they see us return looking healthy, invigorated and happy and see that the run has rejuvenated us, making us more attentive, interested and productive, a better friend, family member and person, they might just cut us some slack. Sometimes, the ends do justify the means.

Sneak in a run!

March

March 1 - A reprieve, New Year's Day has officially moved to March 1st!

Did your Winter get off to a slow start? No problem. Soon after becoming dictator, Julius Caesar decided that the traditional Roman calendar should start in January, not the previously traditional March date. The average January temperature in Rome is around 50 degrees so I guess Julius figured it was a good time of year to make fitness resolutions. I've decided to go back to the pre-Julian calendar so the New Year will start on the backside of Winter. Join me--we will now have time recommit to our failing running resolutions--a fresh start!

Happy New Year, let's run!

March 2 - Stock tip

During recession and times of economic woes, it's not a coincidence that there is strong growth in the sport of running. Perhaps as time and money become more precious, we look at the rock-solid simplicity of running and realize the psychological and physical value offered makes it a safe investment. Not to mention, compared to ski weekends, golf course memberships and keeping polo ponies happy, running can fit into a tight budget. Take stock in running! Another thought-- miles never depreciate--the miles ran in the 70s were 5,280 feet, the same as now . . . even if they seem longer today!

Grab a great deal when you see it, run for broke!

March 3 - Enter a race today, yes, you!

March, the back side of Winter, is the time to heat up our running and focus on the early Spring events! If you have not already, pick an event, enter and commit. A race entry is strong motivation to get in the miles. No yikes about it, people who don't train at all show up and waddle through running events all the time, so no need to get nervous. I'm serious, we all have to start somewhere. Just do it, and the satisfaction of just finishing will be the catalyst for your future running goals! We will party together at the finish line as one big happy fitness community, planting the seeds for those in the sedentary world who watch and stand in awe of those of us having the courage to enter.

Get out the door, you are now in training!

March 4 - One nice late winter day changes everything

All it takes is an almost Spring-like day with a bit of sunshine and the running fire roars to life, but be cautious not to get burned! This is an easy time to do too much too soon. Be smart, be consistent and the magic will come. Don't increase your mileage over 10 percent per week and stick to alternating hard and easy days. This means on days then off; long days then short; or fast days then slow. You get the idea. Work the core on those easy days and you will be flying this Spring on the roads, trails and at the races!

It's okay to be deluded by one nice day, grab it!

March 5 - Be true to yourself and others

My favorite George Carlin line is, "Have you ever noticed that anybody driving slower than you is an idiot, and anyone going faster than you is a maniac?" (BrainyQuote.com) It's an insightful line into our human nature. Do we have similar thoughts about those who run faster or slower than us, or run more miles per week or less miles per week than us? Not that they are maniacs or idiots, but do we feel perhaps inferior or superior when talking to other runners about their statistics? The reality is that our life circumstances and our bodies are so very different. A mile run for one person may be a greater accomplishment and bring more personal satisfaction than another person finishing a marathon. When we do something heroic or amazing, only we can know for sure that it was. What others observe, say or think about our accomplishments may boost or deflate our egos but it's up to us to be honest and true to ourselves and do what we think we can or should do in this life to be a more complete and better person. The daily run gives us insight on who we are and who we can be. Knowing that our fellow runners are on the same path can make us more tolerant, caring and helpful.

Run, learn, and grow.

March 6 - Read run

I run, I read, I write. I'm a big fan of novels with a running theme. Unfortunately, they are few and far between. My favorite book of all time is *Once a Runner* by John L. Parker. Parker's old-school hardcore running novel captures the essence of training and racing like no other. Every few years it goes back into print and gets reviewed as the greatest running book ever, then it goes out of print and starts selling online as a rare and valuable book. The sequel, *Return to Carthage* is my second-favorite book. I suggest you grab hardcover copies of these books whenever they are in print. Read, keep and cherish these books, even if they become valuable again!

Great running books will get you out the door!

March 7 - When the wind blows

It's time to call in some favors. Get a ride upwind then run home, or drive upwind, leave a car and catch a ride back to get the car whenever. I always enjoy a point to point run because it doesn't seem so pointless. If a ride is not an option, it is smart to run straight into the teeth of the wind as long as you can stand it, knowing that at any time, you can turn around and warm up while being blown home safely.

Get out and set that point-to-point personal record!

March 8 – Run . . . or jump out of a plane

Life can be tough, even when things seem to be going well. Post-holiday depression is a real thing, but even the stress from day-to-day life can lead to a midlife crisis or at least put our mood into a funky dark hole. Yikes! What's the answer? I don't know for sure, but I'd bet something as simple as a bucket list can make a difference. What to put on it? My vote is for a half-marathon, marathon, triathlon, or ultra-marathon, whichever seems the least impossible to do (What did you expect?). Worst case scenario, you will get a clean T-shirt to wear after you finish each of them. Or you could buy a Harley, learn to pole dance or jump out of a plane!

Avoid the crisis and get out for a run!

March 9 - Running sucks

Monday had me feeling tired and low after a long but rewarding Sunday helping put on a race that started with a 4:30 a.m. alarm and ended after a long cleanup and a bit too much celebrating the successful day. I ran out into a very gray 45-degree world with icy rain on muddy, shoe-sucking, flooded trails. I got in 5 very tough miles. On days like these, it takes a seemingly super-human effort to drag ourselves out the door. We head out anyway, knowing that we have chosen a difficult and extreme sport, in fact, a sport that is considered punishment in other sports. We get it, in fact it's the reason we run. I left the house in a bit of a depressed funk and returned feeling heroic. Yes, a hero only to myself but with a powerful lift in my spirits, more than any drug could match. Running sucks and it's fine by me.

Face the suck head on!

March 10 - There is no "only" when it comes to running

When asked how far we ran today or what race we are running next, I'm sure we have all at some time answered, I "only" ran 3 miles, or I'm "only" doing the 5K, or I'm "only" doing the half. I'm here to tell you, NEVER short-change your run, and never give excuses or apologies for any run or race! Every step counts, every run you head out to do is amazing and no matter how it goes, you should be proud of the effort and share your run proudly! Never, use the word "ONLY" when describing your run! On every run, remember that you had the courage to head out the door and do the hard work.

Only run proud!

March 11 - There is no magic

There seems to be no magic when it comes to getting in good running shape, just a lot of tough miles on the way. Once the fitness arrives, there often seems to be a breakthrough run that can only be described as magical, fast, effortless, and glorious! Until the fitness arrives, hang tough.

Today's run might be magic. There's only one way to find out.

March 12 - How is your form?

The most common mistake is over-striding. A long stride results with a hard heal strike, causing the runner to break their forward movement and create impact that can lead to many common running injuries. Cutting the stride in half cuts the impact and the motions of the joints to almost zero. By shortening stride and striking midfoot, the runner can run with lighter, less controlling footwear. How to tell if you are over-striding? If you wear your heels down quickly you most likely over-stride. You can check this by counting one arm swings during one minute of running. If you get to 80 or more, your stride will be about right. It may feel like shuffling, so shuffle fast!

Now you have something to think about on today's run, get out there!

March 13 - It often seems our running has plateaued

I can remember the first few months when I started running and how I hit what seemed like a barrier in my progress. I could never run more than 20 miles per week without being sidelined with some new pain. About a year into my running, I remember 30 miles per week seemed to be the maximum mileage without some new issue. A couple of years later I was struggling with getting past 40 miles per week when it finally sunk in--running was not the problem; it was how I put in the miles. I had learned how to run 20 then 30 then 40 miles per week with the body I had. I had learned what workouts I could or could not get away with. I learned when to run hard and when to take a day off. I learned to run 40 miles per week pain-free and I keep learning.

Run, learn, then run even more.

March 14 - Make your run a priority

Stop the habit of running when you have time (no one has time). Plan the time you run. For the workouts to get done, they need to be scheduled. Put your daily run in your appointment calendar and give it the same priority as any other scheduled meeting. When a friend invites you to dinner at 7 p.m. on a night you have scheduled a 6:30 p.m. run, explain that you have a late appointment but you can make it at 8 p.m. or perhaps another night. (You are not lying, your run is on the schedule, just don't mention the run part!) Is the run selfish? No, being depressed or having a heart attack or stroke due to lifestyle are just a few reasons a run that gives back so much for the time invested is not selfish.

Take the time to run, so you can be there for others in the long run.

March 15 - When we feel as bad as the weather, hang tough

Yesterday I headed out for a dreary, rainy run with my body feeling worse than the weather--tired, dead legged and stiff. I gutted it out for a while then made a turn so it would be a short loop back to home. Twenty minutes into this torture and a block from home, the pain magically faded, and I imagined the sun was breaking out (But it was only getting darker and wetter). I felt light on my feet, smooth, and the running was effortless. I took a turn away from home and into the woods where my short run turned long and my day was made. The moral to the story--yes, it's the same old story!

Hang tough on your run and the magic might just come.

March 16 - If all our friends ran

I had a wonderfully philosophic conversation with an old friend today on a long, socially fulfilling run. The thought occurred, if all my friends ran, it would be fun and efficient catching up like this. Taking it a step further, if all our business meetings and negotiations could take place on the run, and if we were the most-fit people at the meeting, we could pick up the pace when we want to get in the last word!

Run today so this can happen.

March 17 - May you have the luck of the Irish

The St. Pats runs are a sure sign the Spring race season is on. I'm sure many of you took advantage and shook out the winter legs. Whatever pace you ran, it should only excite you to know that you will get faster as the season wears on, but only if you stay pain-free. Don't up the miles too fast and don't run into any pain that seems to be increasing as you run. Just bail-- there is no room for ego in this sport, and no room for a rigid schedule or bull-headedness. Yes, a beautiful Spring day off may seem more painful than any run you could have done, but it's the reality of our sport. I repeat the important stuff.

If you are pain free, get out there!

March 18 - Traffic jams can suck . . . or not

First, be prepared in life for anytime a run might be an option by keeping a set of run gear in the car or at work. When stuck in a nightmare traffic jam, don't pound the steering wheel and swear. Instead, smile, park the car, put on your gear and get in a run. You will not be losing any time in your day! The traffic will most likely be gone when you finish and your arrival time will not vary by much. Make the smart and happy choice.

Always choose happiness and always be ready to run.

March 19 - Running, such a simple sport

Running, on the surface, is such a simple, uncomplicated sport that is fulfilling both physically and mentally. With just minimal equipment and even less athletic ability, you can't get any more basic. Running truly is just one foot in front of the other, and as they say, even a child can do it. As we mature into our running, the positive aspects of its addictive qualities take over, and we slide below the surface of this so-called simple activity and find there is an ocean of information to be learned. We can delve into the hundreds of running books, monthly periodicals and laboratory reports on physiology, gait analysis, nutritional needs and so much more that has been written. Then again, we can just enjoy our simple runs! The truth is, we learn the most during our runs.

Run, learn and enjoy each mile of today's run, at whatever level.

March 20 - Don't listen to the demons

When the voices in your head get together and decide you should do anything other than run, stop thinking and go run. Show your mind that not running is not an option and the thoughts in there are wasting their time. "Hey head, get with the program or be miserable, I'm running!" If you feel bad; rundown, or unmotivated, that's good--you know you are running anyway and once this run is finished you will have a much greater feeling of satisfaction and accomplishment than an easy run on a nice day, Ha! You beat the demons!

Shut up demons, I have to run!

March 21 - New running shoes

I got a new pair of running shoes today and can't wait to put in some miles. Not only do I like trying on a bunch of shoes and talking to the running store staff about my options, but new running shoes bring a slew of positive thoughts, feelings and motivation. Fresh shoes, fresh legs, new goals, new run plans, race plans and thoughts of roads and trails I can't wait to try them on. New running shoes are an investment with immediate and immeasurable returns, even while still in the box!

Shop, make plans, run, and get those new shoes dirty.

March 22 - When Spring finally springs

They seem to bloom like wildflowers, runners taking to the streets on the first fair-weather days. For those of us who have kept our winter outdoor running vigil alive through sleet, gale force wind, snow and dark of night, it's hard to hide our smug feelings of superiority and satisfaction as we wave and say hello. Ha! The truth is, what we put into and take from our running is very personal and we don't really know what that runner we see out there is experiencing. Perhaps they are taking those first brave and nervous steps into the fitness world and are about to get the satisfaction we experienced when we finally got up the courage to start. Bravo and a high five to all.

Get out there and give them all a thumbs up!

March 23 - You are not a running god

When we are upping our weekly mileage, which happens a lot this time of year, it's hard to not get excited and move the fitness level up a notch, often doing too much, too soon. We are flirting with the edge whenever we move up the miles from a base amount our body has adapted to, so, when you are feeling like a running god and your body seems to be able to handle all you are throwing at it, the reality is that it's most likely time to take the day off or put in an easy run--dang. If it seems too good to be true, trust that thought. Don't you just hate being mortal?

A day off can save you a month off, so run smart today.

March 24 - Rain, rain go away--NOT!

I just returned from a weekend in Atlanta, Georgia where it rained non-stop. So, needless to say, each day's run was in the rain and as I headed out into the gloom, I grew to realize I loved it! Pounding into a hard rain adds adventure and a sense of combat with the elements. Once finished, a run in the rain gives back a sense of satisfaction much bigger than the sum of its parts. Yes, only a run in the rain requires you to open the door and go for it while the rest of the world looks sadly through the window.

Every run is an adventure, go have one.

March 25 - The courage to start

Running is a personal sport; nobody else cares about our race times, our weekly mileage or our running pace. That said, nothing about lining up for a race should make us feel nervous or self-conscious. But for many of us, no matter how many times we toe the line, those feelings creep in. I understand how entering an event for the first time can be perceived as an almost insurmountable challenge for the beginning runner. When we finally leave our comfort zone and take the plunge, we find that the fears or preconceived ideas of racing were silly, holding us back from the full enjoyment of the sport.

Run, race and experience all running has to offer.

March 26 - Look and feel fast

Every sport has its own look, from the Orvis catalogue persona of the fly fisherman to the black leather and colors of a motorcycle gang. As with each sport, the look comes from the performance products used by the participants. The look of the runner comes from apparel and footwear that make us efficient, fast, comfortable and injury-free--products that work. I'm keen to pick out runners in any crowd as the run-specific brands are dead giveaways. Who else but a runner would be styling in brightly colored footwear from Saucony, Brooks or Altra when they could get a sporty look from $50 Nike models made specifically for

Wal-Mart? I'm sure only a runner would feel comfortable in public wearing neon-colored CEP compression sleeves.

Get the look, these colors run!

March 27 - Don't let a good economy keep you from running

It's a busy life and there are a million things competing with our time. It is said that when the economy is good and people have extra cash, they buy new toys like boats, motorcycles, large TVs, vacation homes, and other things that take up our free time and take away from the precious time we have for our health. Our bodies can easily get put on the back burner as we get distracted by stuff that gets old quickly, and can get in the way of the daily run as we move it around or try to peddle it. Consider this a heads up, a reminder of how easy it is to lose what is precious, your running, to what is less important--things.

Keep your run, your sanity and your fitness first.

March 28 - Run smart or don't run

I repeat the important stuff. Fifty degrees and sunny-- a tempting day for a run, especially for those of us who are putting in a few too many miles too soon, and perhaps are dealing with a twinge of training pain besides. Dang. The hardest but smartest part of our sport is to not run a planned workout, especially when we are obsessed with weekly mileage targets and especially when the run you should skip is your long run. "But I am following a schedule and have a race coming up in 3 weeks!" You can't race at all if you are injured or sick, but you can race rested and perhaps a bit under-trained. Skip the run, work on the core, get a massage, ice any suspicious-feeling parts of the body and come back with only a short easy run when it seems safe, maybe in a day or two.

Get out for a . . . walk.

March 29 - A time to play, a time to work

As part of the fitness community, I'm sure you can relate; the weekend left me sore, tired and pleasantly beat to a pulp. It included a glorious long run along with a marathon of other physical and non-physical, non-stop action. I often find that getting back to work gives me a chance to recover from play and that productive time behind my desk (with my shoes off) has its place. Come to think of it, thanks to play, what I'm doing at my desk on Mondays does not fit with the word "work." It's really part of my running life, a recovery day.

A time to run, a time to work--I mean recover.

March 30 - Training schedule? What schedule?

It's a beautiful morning for a run and . . . I'm taking the day off. Dang, it's hard to run smart. Yesterday I had twinges of pain all over the place on the run, with my body telling me to take a day off, but the schedule saying otherwise. Schedules will get you in trouble ALL the time. Never consider a schedule the authority; they are just a guide to help you make progress. Lots of knowledge and science goes into some schedules but they are a static view of a dynamic venture. It might even be good to get off-schedule a bit, right from the beginning, just to let it know who's really calling the shots! It's so easy to read this but going off-schedule is often the hardest thing we will do as runners with a plan. It gives us a feeling of failure and wimping out, when the reality is that getting out for the run would be our failure.

That said, if you are healthy, go run for me!

March 31 - Know when to fold 'em, know when to run

I just ran 10 days in a row, running much higher mileage than usual, day after day pushing myself past what I would consider sensible training. I was not alternating hard and easy runs as I normally do, but running in a way that I would not call smart. To my amazement, I seemed to be getting stronger each day. I had the thought that I was like a gambler on a roll, which made me pull my chips off the table and take my winnings. I took 2 days completely off and followed it up with a short run and another day off. I'm back to my normal conservative buildup and the running is going well. What did I learn? Nothing I would suggest. I'm sure I was close to dodging a bullet, but how close? This sport continues to baffle me after all these years and I think it' just one of the many aspects of running that keeps me passionate and in the game. Dig it.

May your run baffle you.

April

April 1 - Much more than a run

When feeling happy, heading out for a run increases the joy; on the flip side, a good run can also chase away the blues. The run is one of life's great coping tools, truly a gift to those of us who run. When the bombs went off at the Boston Marathon, we headed out and ran. Grief shared is grief diminished. We shared solidarity on solitary runs around the country. Recently I listened to a tragic news story of 19 firefighters killed in the line of duty. I headed out to run--to think and dedicate my run.

Dedicate today's run, run for them.

April 2 - Don't let this day get away

This wonderful life can turn south on a dime. One day you run a PR, the next you can lose a job, be diagnosed with a wicked disease or get killed in an accident. No, I have not had anything tragic happen in my life lately but I'm just throwing out a reminder of why every healthy day is a gift and should be cherished. Lace em' up, get outside and live life to the max. When the bad days come, we'll be ready to rest.

But not today!

April 3 - You are the perfect runner

We live in a world obsessed with weight, body image, and diets. Along with this fixation, the numbers of people fighting anorexia, bulimia and the money spent on weight loss products, diets and fat reduction surgery has grown exponentially. As runners and walkers, we are far from immune to this obsession and the many negative and even dangerous and addictive aspects of it. It's not like we don't know this stuff, but I find it helpful to be reminded so we can take stock and be honest with ourselves. Weight comes down to calories consumed, calories burned and the genetically pre-disposed bodies we have. Forget body image and learn to love the body you have and appreciate the differences between us all.

Fast or slow, love yourself and love today's run.

April 4 - What's today's excuse?

After the brutality of an endless Winter, we hardly need a motivational push out the door to get in the run. The reality is that we will quickly forget the cold and start blaming the heat, our busy lives or whatever excuse we need to knock back the priority of our daily run. It takes constant diligence to remember that our health is everything and the run is a big part of it, not just the run itself but the healthy changes in lifestyle we make due to our commitment. We all know how easy it is to lose focus when we are not facing a health crisis, then one day, we wake to see a person in the mirror we never thought we'd be.

Look in the mirror, then promise that person you will always get out that door.

April 5 - It's all good

I enjoy the hype and excitement of the premier events, they give credibility to our sport and allow us to line up with the world's best--a bit behind them maybe--but there is something magical about knowing we are toeing the same starting line and racing the same course. Cool stuff. That said, rounding it out by entering the small, down-home, grassroots events seems good for the soul. Train alone, train with a partner and balance your year's event calendar with variety. Diversification keeps us motivated, excited and gives us back more than the sum of its parts.

That said, my favorite run is my daily run, today's run!

April 6 - Discover who you are and who you might be

While playing (running) in the woods this morning, I was again reminded that running really is play time, an escape from the so called "important" activities of this adult life. Running gives us time to be ageless, a time to put our mind, body and soul into an activity with little practical value. NOT! The late runner-philosopher Dr. George Sheehan once said, "When we take to the roads, we place ourselves in a setting that fosters our art--which is no less than the self we make and the life we live." (From the book *Personal Best*, chapter 10, by George Sheehan, M.D., 1989.)

Get on the path of discovery, get out that door.

April 7 - Winter makes us tough, or does it?

After a hard Winter of running outdoors, warm Spring days rock. The temptation is to strip off the layers and run a bit underdressed for the temperature. The reality is that the warm days are coming and heat adaptation will become important. A good way to start is to overdress a bit on cool days. It's tempting to run in shorts just because you can, but overdressing a bit on the cool days will pay off as the warm days hit. Heat is a serious enemy you can't dress for and need to respect; getting the body heat adapted will make you seriously tough.

Today, dress and run for later success.

April 8 - Get your groove on

Variety is the spice of running. Try to get in 3 types of runs each week--one hard-paced difficult run, maybe on hills, and one very long run that takes you near your physical limits. The rest can be comfortable runs to enjoy all the sights and sounds of the world around you while still getting the work done and putting miles in the log. Each run will complement the others; the long runs takes the stress out of getting out the door for any shorter distance, and the hard runs are good for your confidence. Get out of the rut.

Mix it up today.

April 9 - Listen to your body

This is a common expression that makes some sense. I say jokingly, listen to your body, except when you are in a race! The reality is that when you push to your limits, you and your body become enemies, one fighting to keep the hammer down and one fighting to get you to stop. The trick is to discern what is truly dangerous behavior and what is just the pain of fatigue that you can push through; hence, time to ignore the body. When the balance of pain and effort get us to the finish line with a new personal record and a great sense of fulfillment, it is important to savor the moment, and reflect on all you did to arrive at this point. Think about days you got in the miles when the last thing you wanted to do was get up and run. This run was your best. Don't allow negative thoughts to spoil the moment, like what you could have done better in training, or runs that you missed. Today, you are perfect, the numbers prove this out. A good effort can brighten our lives and carry us forward. There are times I think back to a great run, reliving the feeling years later and finding I can still take pride and pleasure from it. Life will throw darks days our way, some overwhelming, but by savoring the good days, the memories will be a part of our arsenal of thoughts that can pull us through.

Don't listen to your lazy body, get out the door and run!

April 10 - Diversify your fitness portfolio

For sanity's sake, we all need more than one passion. It's like having insurance or a diversified portfolio. When something happens and we can't pursue our obsession, we must have an option or, YIKES! May I suggest a well-rounded portfolio of three passions, or should I say one obsession and 2 passions? The terms are close to interchangeable, but life without one activity where you go all in and over the line will leave you in the middle of the road--blah. Ideally, you could have two physical passions and one that you can pursue with most of your parts not working. I'm talking about writing, reading, research or what have you. As for physical, it needs to be aerobic and able to cop you a few endorphins, such as biking, swimming or paddle sports. These thoughts came up while I was on the bike a lot the last two weeks because of a running pain. I was trying to be PATIENT DAMMIT! Anyway, I'm back on my feet and getting in miles this week, whew.

Get out and run, then do something else!

April 11 - Even when we run smart, stuff happens

For those of us who are upping our miles slowly and doing all we can to run smart, issues can slowly sneak in. We may get up in the morning with a bit of a sore heel, arch, hip or perhaps knee. The kind of pains that go away as we warm up and get moving. I call these pains warning shots, reminding us to ice and run a few easy days. If a pain comes up during the run, feel it out for just a bit to see if it's fleeting; if it increases even the slightest bit, stop the run, walk home or get a ride, ice, and take several days off. If you follow this strategy, you have a good chance of dodging the long-term recovery bullet. What I've just explained is the hardest part of being a runner, which is not finishing the planned run or race. Someday, the reward will come, just not today. I keep repeating the important stuff in Spring.

DNF = Did Nothing Foolish

April 12 - SEE, Running is good for you!

I, like many, am a sucker for studies that show positive results for the stuff I do. Some examples would be: drinking red wine, eating dark chocolate and of course, running! The latest one shows a huge reduction in glaucoma and another shows a reduction of cataracts for those who run. Looks like I get to keep all of my vices and my eyesight!

So, all you chocoholic wine snobs (like me) --run, then reward yourself!

April 13 - We share the run

There is so much more to each of us than meets the eye. We all live rich and interesting lives and have valuable stories to tell. As we go through our day-to-day lives we pass people on the street, they drive by in cars, they surround us in crowds--people we don't know a thing about, people we most likely take for granted. It's hard to remember at times that each of them are special, perhaps they are the most amazing person we could ever meet, if given that privilege. A thought occurred to me as I lined up with several thousand runners at the starting line of a marathon. Here I was in a crowd of mostly strangers and I realized that I was not taking them for granted. In fact, it felt strangely like they were my friends. It struck me that I knew some important things about each of them. I knew they had the guts to toe the marathon starting line and that they had set and were about to accomplish a long-term goal. They had managed their time, trained and lived, in at least some ways, similar lives to mine. We smiled and made eye contact as we went through our pre-race thoughts and rituals. Not strangers but fellow runners sharing the road, sharing our pain, and soon our success.

May today's run bring the world closer together.

April 14 - Spring, dig it!

For those of you who slogged through the Winter miles, it's time to reap. For the rest of us, its time get out and jiggle the fat. These Spring days get no better--cool mornings, glorious days and the risk of overdoing it. Sorry, I repeat the important stuff. Seriously, there is no safe way to zoom into shape; the only way to get there injury-free is to creep up the miles. I know the roads and trails are calling but I believe the 10 percent rule is golden. If you ran 20 total miles last week, this week should not be over 22. The weekly long run can be bumped up about a mile per week. Do you have time to get ready for that half-marathon in June? Do the math from where you are now, figure out the race date, enter, then get out the door.

Patience sucks, that's why they invented Ibuprofen, so go run!

April 15 - Run away from it

Ah, the good old hunter and gatherer days! Today's life is busy, complex and stressful. The daily run lets us shed off the mental load as the miles add up. The head clears from 1,000 thoughts at once down to a singularly clear mission of movement. What would we do without running, this simple, physical and psychological gift? No need to think about it, unplug and hit the run reset button, peace is just a few fast steps past that door.

Run like days of old, chase down dinner!

April 16 - Choose wisely

When it comes to a healthy lifestyle, set yourself up for success. Examples: Either a long weekend in Vegas or hiking in Yellowstone; a dinner out at Porky's Rib House or a vegan brew pub; a long walk after dinner with friends or cigars and more drinks. Most often, the healthy choice is not a difficult one to make and not a lesser choice at any level. You might have to take the lead when it comes to a healthy choice with friends or family but no matter what kind of backlash you might get, it's only a knee-jerk reaction from years of bad decisions. Bad decisions may at first may sound more fun but once the reality of how alive they feel doing the good stuff sets in, you'll be off the hook. So take the hit and get your way, eventually, you will be appreciated and will move up a notch in their book.

Your success starts with choosing to run today, get on it!

April 17 - We have found running and now we are runners

No longer do we just want to run, we need to run. Our need for running is a need to get outside, perhaps a need to get to the woods. Running is our natural fix. Running is a place we go to recharge the body and mind, like an ancient druid that gets supernatural powers from contact with the earth, we draw clarity and energy with each footfall. A walk in the woods works wonders; add sweat and it's like throwing on the holy water, cleansing us from deep in our soul to the surface of our skin. Perhaps the need to run comes from the get-down-to-basics nature of our sport. Running is so unlike the complicated, computer-generated framework that has come to control much of our daily existence. We are beautifully simple-- runners.

Fulfill those needs. Eat, drink, sleep, love and run today.

April 18 - Need a bit of sympathy?

It's amazing how differently we can feel both physically and mentally at different times during the same run. We live for the magic runs that are effortless from the first step to the last, leaving us fired up for the next time out. That said, more often we start out dragging, breathing hard and feeling heavy and tired. Usually it takes a few miles for the body to groove in, so no matter how bad it starts, we can be patient--miserable but patient. We are rewarded as our heart rate drops and our steps become light . . . but not always. We may head out rested and ready to get in a good solid effort and for no reason our bodies head South. We may battle the demons for a while only to end up in a walk. We may try and the body will have none of it. We struggle home, hoping for a change in biorhythms or whatever, but they don't come. Hopefully tomorrow will rock. So much for motivation, eh?

Get out the door, this may be your day, or, it may be tomorrow. Yes, I keep saying this.

April 19 - Running has given us everything

We rely on our bodies to pursue our sport; to the runner, the body and mind are one. I believe this gives us an advantage over sedentary Americans, those who take the body for granted, often ignoring diet and health in pursuit of what--success and happiness? All the intelligence and wealth in the world cannot give us what running does. Take a look at the physical condition of leaders of industry, Washington politicians and corporate ladder climbers. Many seem to have sacrificed health to succeed. The moral of the story is that a degree from Harvard, Yale, or anywhere, plus all the ambition in the world, without the understanding of a decent 10K personal best (or at least a passion for some sport) won't get them what we've got!

Live, love, learn, earn and run, today.

April 20 - Patriot's Day

Another Boston Marathon has happened or will go in the books soon with tens of thousands of runners thumbing their noses at terrorism and living life free and Boston Strong. The terrorists failed; we are not terrified. For all of us, every time we head out the door it is a victory, we show the world our great life in America won't be stopped. Kind of like saying, "Hey all you cowardice punks, you have already lost this war, perhaps you should quit wasting your time and energy and crawl back in your hole!"

We run as one.

April 21 - Don't worry, you'll forget about it! (From my daughter Anna)

My forgetfulness is a gift to my running life. There are routes, races and hills that ended with me swearing "Never again," and sore days that made me question why I would do this to myself. Somehow, the next day the shoes still go on and out the door I go. I have to thank this running amnesia for pushing the negative memories back and reminding me that what I did was AWESOME, pain be damned. The next time you finish a run and say "never again," smile, and remember you'll forget you ever said it. So, tackle the big hill or add on the extra 5 miles you KNOW you want to try. It might suck but hey . . . you'll forget about it and do it again someday.

Go get in a painful run you will soon forget.

April 22 - Unplug, run and reset

News stories of civil war, natural disasters and political conflict seem to compete with the mental energy needed to get through the normal day-to-day difficulties of life, like bills, family issues and health. It's more essential than ever that we shut it all down, lace em up, and blast out the door into the natural world. Our daily run allows us to refresh our brain and body like a much-needed shower, ready to take on the world again. The headlines give us reason to make the daily run a priority.

Run and refuel so you can move forward.

April 23 - It's all about risk and rewards

An active lifestyle comes with risk, but also great rewards. That said, a sedentary life is also risky, especially when you take into account medical issues that stem from lack of activity and psychological issues like boredom. I often say jokingly, "run fast and take chances." My context for this line always has to do with distance and speed, not personal safety. An example of taking chances is pushing oneself to the limit in a race or running faster or farther than you think you can.

Compared to most sports, running is a safe choice, but we all need to keep safety in mind. When we head out the door, bad things can happen to us. By running smart we can avoid most of them. Wear bright clothing and always run against traffic. If running at night, light yourself up with strobe lights, a reflective vest and a head lamp. Never trust a car, bike or pedestrian and expect the unexpected, look both ways and be aware. Look for safe routes and only wear ear buds in areas closed to traffic of any kind. Have great respect for the weather and adjust your run route, clothing and hydration accordingly, especially in extreme heat. The great rewards will come--lower blood pressure, increased self-efficacy, reduced risk of heart disease, more energy and the list goes on!

Get out, run safe and reap the rewards.

April 24 - There is no shortcut to the finish line

We all know the type--people who are always looking for immediate gratification, shortcuts, get-rich-quick schemes, miracle diets, pills to reduce fat, seemingly anything that does not require hard work, discipline or patience. It's easy to avoid these kinds of people, just hang around with people who run. We thrive on no shortcuts to success, just long tough miles and only ourselves to cheat. Honest and straightforward butt-kicking hard work, with a guaranteed return on the energy invested, every time. There is no faking it!

Get out there for a hard and honest run you will be proud of.

April 25 - Don't let ego get in the way of the fun

When we start to compare our running with someone else's we are asking for trouble. We all have different genetic makeups, health histories and life experiences, no two people are alike. Three miles might be a fulfilling long distance for one person and it might be 30 miles for another. I plan to set goals and training schedules that will be fulfilling to me and applaud all people who have reached their personal running goals whatever they might be. Let's crush ego and experience a new-found feeling of freedom and self-fulfillment!

Today's run will be perfect, perfect for you as you are right this minute.

April 26 - Always be ready to run

Way too often I hear the words," I wish I had my running stuff with me." It may be at a conference where there's an unexpected 2-hour break or at an airport where a plane is delayed by hours or when a car won't start or dies on the road 5 miles from where you need to be in an hour. In this modern life, we rely on things to work and happen as expected way too much. Yes, cars are more reliable and the cell phone is our new answer to getting a ride or killing time, but getting in an unexpected run can be far more memorable and rewarding. Let's put it on our to-do lists today! I am packing a basic running kit to leave in my car, at work under my desk and for my airplane carry-on bag. The next time we meet, we will have great stories to tell about an amazing, unexpected run.

Run when you have the chance, like now!

April 27 - Raining and perfect

No warm Spring days in sight but the temperatures have been great for getting in the run--yes, some splashing around in puddles, but heck, we are lucky to have a sport that gets us outside and smiling while much of the world whines about the weather. Let's get out there and take in the sights, sounds and smells of Spring while enjoying these 50-something degree days!

Run right through those puddles!

April 28 - Tricks to make the long run shorter

One trick I sometimes use is to show up early and run a couple of miles before joining friends for our usual 5-

mile run. Sneaking in miles can not only make a longer run seem easy, but it will give you a smug feeling of superiority--just don't mention it or show it! A similar way to get in your long run is to include a race in your total mileage. Pick a race you are not serious about and plan your long run around it. Perhaps run 4 miles before lining up at the start of a 10K. Doing the last 6 in the race setting can make for a motivational finish. You will find it a huge mental advantage running along with people who are only at mile 3 knowing you are at already at mile 7 of your own 10-mile secret event! You are a running god!

Make the run fun but don't gloat . . . well, maybe just a little.

April 29 - You are a running rock star!

According to U.S. Running Trends Report from *Running USA*, America's running registrations in 2017 remained consistent with the total registrants in 2016. In 2017, there were a total of nearly 18.3 million registrants, down just slightly from 18.5 million in 2016. (RunningUSA.org)

Knowing that less than 5 percent of Americans enter a running race each year is a darn good reason to feel good about your level of fitness. You rock! Unfortunately, most of us compare our running to the top one percent, the elite runners, instead of exceptional mortal runners, diminishing our amazing personal achievements. Did I mention that you rock! But don't slip into the other 95 percent of the population, ever, or the world will know! Actually, the world couldn't care less, your running is yours alone. But you'll know!

Get your less-than-5-percent butt out there and run!

April 30 - Don't squander the gift

The serenity of the run continues to smooth out the roller coaster of emotions and setbacks in life. The fact that we found running is a true gift. Every healthy running day is precious; we must keep vigilant to stay in a state of health that allows us to take full advantage of the gift. Let's eat smart, train smart, race smart and do the core work to make this happen, not just to help ourselves but to be better prepared to help the world!

Run smart, run today, run forever.

May

May 1 - Great job out there!

Often in a race we are so caught up with our own experience that it's easy to forget that in every event we enter, we are surrounded by people accomplishing amazing personal goals, perhaps heroic feats! Finishing times and place don't tell much of a story, only the runner knows the effort it took to get to the starting line. They may have lost 100 pounds or are running again after years of recovery from a near-death accident, or perhaps their run is a celebration, a return to a normal life after a struggle with loss and grief. Their run may be the culmination of the long road back from addiction or any personal struggle, we just don't know. Even if it's not a life-changing effort, perhaps just a personal best from putting in the training and reaping the reward from the effort, each runner has a story and we are playing a part in it as we race together. We never know when our words of encouragement or just a clap or cheer will bring a tear to an eye and joy to a heart. When we race, we are all in it together, on the home team, pushing each other to greatness!

Train today, cheer tomorrow.

May 2 - Run away from a virus

The daily run not only gives us a place to escape the torrent of bad news for a bit, but has also helped prepare us for a pandemic. The following comes from an article from *Runner's World* by Heather May Irvine, April 28, 2020. "There's no question that the immune system weakens with age, but running might actually slow down the aging process. Specifically, it seems to strengthen the adaptive (or acquired) immune system, according to Caroline Jouhourian, M.D., gastroenterologist at Lowell General Hospital in Massachusetts."

The article continues, "The adaptive immune system is learned over time, meaning it creates antigens to fight specific infections. That means, according to James Turner, Ph.D., immunobiology specialist from University of Bath, U.K., older adults who are active might respond better to vaccines. A 2014 paper published in *Brain, Behavior, and Immunity* supports this idea: Short bouts and long-term exercise 'significantly augments the immune response to vaccination.'"

Have a great, proactive run today!

May 3 - Just say no to birthdays and yes to parties and long celebration runs

Birthdays are a celebration of life so why let age get in the way? After one hits adulthood, the actual age of a person is not relevant. Actually, keeping track of your age can be detrimental. You are either too young or too old, by just mentioning your age you open yourself up to age discrimination either way. Better to be judged by your accomplishments along the way and how consistently you run out the door. Peter Pan had it right!

You are ageless, you are free, go run.

May 4 - Bring it on

Not all days are created equal, some slip by and are forgotten, then there are those pearls, days etched into our memory for us to savor for a lifetime. Event days can often fit the bill, perhaps even adding to our meaning of life. If you have trained and planned for a long race, don't be stressed or disappointed by a bad weather forecast. Keep in mind, finishing a race on a horrible day won't be boring and soon forgotten. Crossing a finish line in adverse conditions can be powerful and at the very least memorable! We plan, we train, we set goals then on race day we live life in full color: we find out who we are and who we might be. These are days of self-discovery, valuable days indeed, pearls. Savor every minute, especially when the conditions are fierce, the clock is running and your performance is nothing short of heroic.

Savor today's run.

May 5 – Run, but just to the crumbling edge

I strained my calf in a trail race a month ago, keeping me away from the daily run until these past few days. Luckily, I could bike and swim and my diversified fitness portfolio lessened the pain of the time away from my true love. I inched my way back and now can run 4 miles with no sign of a problem. Amen. This return to running after the break brought on flashbacks to the time I started putting in miles for the first time and the passion ran high. This feeling was a reminder that I may have been taking the daily run and my fitness level for granted. Injury is a harsh reminder of how precious the run is and that we need to run smart and within ourselves, somewhere just this side of that crumbling edge.

Run hard but respect the limits.

May 6 - Savor the pain

The weekly long run is always an adventure, never knowing how we'll feel in the late, valuable miles. All the running before the fatigue hits are necessary but the miles that start to hurt are what we came for, the good stuff! These painful miles are where the body learns to store more glycogen and better utilize oxygen--the training effects we're looking for. Savor the pain and get excited when it hits. You worked hard to get here and to feel this bad; the rewards will come!

Run, scream, finish and smile.

May 7 - Every Breath is a Gift

The yoga gang is big on focusing on being in the moment, forgetting what has happened or all that will happen and truly experiencing what is happening. It's a busy and complicated life we choose, rich with goals and experiences, a life that often requires an effort on our part to be in the moment. Yoga does it with a visual point of focus and concentration on deep breaths and poses, stopping the endless chatter of the brain and getting down to basics. I call it the yoga buzz. Running helps us experience being in the moment by immersing us in the sights, sounds and smells of the world as we pass thought it, feeling the wind on our face, the heat, the cold, and the wet. When we run, we use our muscles and core strength and fire up the nerves that serve the brain-to-foot coordination, making it hard not to live in the moment. Amen! As Webster defines it: Amen: Used to express solemn ratification (as of an expression of faith) or hearty approval (as of an assertion). Yeah baby!

Run in the moment, now. Amen.

May 8 – The courage to start, again

We miss a few days of running, this turns into a week of not running, then . . . a slippery slope that can take us to no running at all and a gray cloud that hangs over us as we are reminded daily, when we see runners out there, that we are off the wagon. If getting back to the run was easy, I would not be writing this. The time we put aside for the run gets swallowed by a busy life and our loss of fitness becomes a barrier of pain we know will be in front of us when we attempt to run again. So, what will get us back to being a runner? Courage. Remember, you had the courage to start, the courage is within you to start again.

Start again, smile, hurt, and be proud.

May 9 - Racing can get in the way of our running

I love my daily run and everything it does for me. I also love the experience of giving it my all on race day and being totally spent. Long races require tapering down before the race, then recovery days after, cutting into the joy of my daily runs, which creates a dilemma. Not a big deal when it comes to shorter events, but when running a marathon, it's time away from our love. I'm reminded of this today as I savor the soreness from last weekend's race with a short run rather than hitting the trail for longer miles I'd like to get in on this glorious day--darn. A strange thought, that my running can keep me from my running . . . I wish all of life's dilemmas offered such fun choices. Get out and savor today.

Enjoy whatever miles you get in.

May 10 - Those darn long-term goals take quite a commitment!

If you are considering running a Fall marathon, especially your first one, it may sound early to make the commitment, but it's time--yikes! Those darn long-term goals take quite a commitment, but the payback is huge, perhaps life-changing. Marathon training requires time management but the upside is you will find that you are more productive and more responsible with family and work than when you were just drifting along. Busy people do everything, and people who do nothing have no time to do anything. Yes, you don't have time to do this, but commit and you will find it, I promise. Your schedule may look stupid to someone--someone not as smart as you! Did I mention commitment?

You can do this, but need to start today!

May 11 - Hurts so good

Why do we take our bodies to the limit, to the point that we insult our senses, even to a state of pain and panic? Just asking ourselves these questions is cathartic. I'm sure that as we contemplate why, a

plethora of responses shakes loose and starts to flow-
-passion, obsession, nirvana, the chance to feel
complete, fully alive and firing on all cylinders, living
life in full color, out near the crumbling edge. Knowing,
understanding and controlling the fulfillment of the
moment that we have created for ourselves is
incredible. Amen.

Run to the limit, now!

May 12 - The outcome of your run may be pre-determined

I make a point of writing just after I run, with the rush
of fresh endorphins sparking the creative juices. It
seems to make sense, and perhaps the post-run mind
gains insights that it would not get at rest. So, I just
finished a terrible run, 6 miles that turned into 3 miles
with a bad stomach and feeling like I had cotton
shoved in my lungs. A horrid run on a beautiful day in
the woods; at least I had the day going for me. As I
write this I realize I'm happy I got out the door and got
this run out of the way. A thought that just occurred to
me is that perhaps we have bad runs planted in our
bodies and they must come out, like evil spirits.

Get out there and find what kind of run your body has
planned for you today!

May 13 - You are an athlete

This running world of ours includes athletes with incredible abilities and amazing accomplishments, from Olympians to world record holders. Runners who train over 100 miles per week, some who run 100-mile races in less than 24 hours, runners who run faster than our personal best times at every distance in their daily training. That said, the non-runner may wonder why we even get out of bed to put in a 4-mile run at what might be back of the pace as we train for our next event. The answer, as you all know, is that our running is all about us and because when we train and race, we actually have an intimate understanding of what the best runners in the world do, because we do what they do. When we line up and race a personal best time, even if we come in close to last in the event, every training mile seems worth the effort and we savor OUR victory. The runners in front of us do not demoralize us, they inspire us and yes, we inspire them. It's a running thing those outside our world will never understand until they personally run some miles.

I am proud of the run you will get in today.

May 14 - Time, distance, speed and ego

Time, distance and speed are the essence of our sport but they can also be distractions, especially if we worry about how we look on Strava or other social running applications. I had a glorious run today on some very gnarly trails with wicked hills and breathtaking vistas. A 5.3-mile run through ruts and roots at a pace perhaps 2 and a half minutes per mile slower than if I ran down a road. A soul-cleansing, totally fulfilling rave run, that looks lacking on the Garmin from a time, distance and speed aspect. Remember, only you know the real effort you put into today's run.

Don't let ego get in the way of the personal satisfaction of a butt-kicking run.

May 15 - When the long run goes bad

I repeat the important stories. Last week I had a bad long-run experience, not unlike hitting the wall. I finished the last, mentally painful miles at a snail's pace, hoping a car would hit me and put me out of my misery. (Not really but you get the idea.) After a run like this, I find myself afraid to head out the door, nervous to have it happen again. After a bad run, we question why. Are we over-trained, under-trained, is it our diet, stress, depression, bad karma, or perhaps biorhythms? A bad run can be a learning experience, but sometimes, it's just a bad run. No matter the reason, shake it off and be glad you got that one out of the way.

Get back on that horse.

May 16 - Closet triathlete

Okay, I'm an obsessed runner, but have alluded to the fact that I'm a closet triathlete. Today, I've decided to let you peek in the closet. I often refer to a diversified aerobic activities portfolio, a diversification that will keep you sane when your body decides to take some time off from a favorite discipline. Let's say that plantar fascitis does not allow you to run today. Rather than freaking out, not unlike what happens when the market crashes, you head to the pool or get down the bike, let the endorphins roll and these sports suddenly turn to gold! By entering a multi-sport event from time to time, you will enhance your personal perceived value of the other sport disciplines so that even if you are obsessed in one, you can still be fulfilled by another. After my Spring long-target race, I go all in for triathlon, targeting a late Summer race, then, I'm back to 100 percent runner as I get ready for the Fall.

Get out and swim, bike and run, run, run, run.

May 17 - Taper time

For those of you running a long Spring event, the taper is essential but can drive a runner mad. The idle time from backing down the miles is a blessing and a curse. This is a time for the body to lick the wounds and store muscle glycogen. The extra downtime can mess with your head, giving you time to question everything from

94

fitness (am I running enough?) to food (am I eating too much?) to race strategy (how fast should I start?) to obsessing about the weather on race day. Running during your taper sometimes can add fuel to this growing doubt. A short run may feel horrible, leaving you asking, if I feel this bad at 3 miles, how can I possibly finish? If this is how you feel, I can tell you from experience that you are on the right track; those horrible short taper runs mean your body is peaked and ready to pop a big one, seriously. How does this work? That's a good question! Just smile!

Taper, then run fast and take chances.

May 18 - Get back to the land

There is a recurring theme in this book of the positive psychological and physical benefits of the daily run, our daily bread and the value of great running events that keep our running fires lit, events to plan our year around. In light of that, the weekend after Labor Day in Michigan, there is a "far-out" event to put on your bucket list. Run Woodstock is a weekend of trail running in an atmosphere of nature, peace and love. A healing weekend where we can trip back to a bygone age of freedom and fitness, an escape from the reality and trappings of life, where we can camp out on the land and set our souls and inner hippie free. Dig? An endless lineup of classic rock bands and runs, walks (5K, 5M, 10K, 13.1M, 26.2M, 50K, 50M, 100M), yoga and other cool stuff that allows you to create the weekend you need. Our run is normally a precious part of our day, events like this let us experience running at a level above the astral plane, not a part of our day but a weekend celebration of the run. Join me! runwoodstock.com – A shameless plug.

Train today for an event that sets your soul free!

May 19 - Feeling burned out by the daily running grind?

Time to shake things up! Run at the lunch hour or in the evening if you normally run in the morning. Run in the woods if you normally run on the road. Better yet, go run a trail late at night with a headlamp! Start and finish your run at a lake and dive in, perhaps naked! Yikes! Try new shoes, a new route, a new run partner or run with a group. Put a beer out a mile from home. Knowing you get a beer for the cool-down mile may fire you up! Get someone to drop you off a long way from home with no way to get back but to run! Drive to a spot some evening then run home. In the morning, run back and get your car.

You get the idea, now get out there!

May 20 - Life is not fair, and as athletes we are reminded of this often

There are no givens, in training, racing or life. When aiming at a long-term goal we put a lot of life's eggs in one basket--a risk-reward scenario. The risks are high, a lot can happen during several months of training, especially as race week draws near when our bodies are on the edge and susceptible to injury or sickness. We can hope for the best, but need to have a plan for the worst. By reminding ourselves that there is perhaps an 80 percent chance of making it to the starting line, we might train a bit smarter, taking days off when a pain comes up or we are feeling run down. Knowing this, we might be more flexible with our plans, perhaps keeping family and friends intact. The worst-case scenario? Be ready to switch gears 180 degrees when tragedy hits, putting all our effort in a new direction, making a plan for recovery and getting just as focused on the next big comeback as we did for the original plan.

Run smart, run if you should.

May 21 - Beat yourself to a pulp

I love the totally wasted feeling the long run gives me--pleasantly sore, tired, fulfilled and deserving of pure laziness, something a person living in a couch potato haze will never know. I joke that we runners work so hard to feel this bad and we should savor the pain, but the truth is this feeling passes fast, like all good things in life. As we become more fit, it will take a longer or harder run or a tougher course to get this ragged-out feeling back. Bring it on!

Sometimes you just need to take it to the limit.

May 22 - Your own records are meant to be broken

It's a combination of things that get us out the door and running each day. Some that can fire us up big-time are stories of inspiration or broken world records. It's a gift to encounter bigger-than-life people living and performing on the edge, way beyond our comfort zone. When we read about someone running 2:02 for a marathon or a full distance IRONMAN® in just over 8 hours, or someone running a 7-minute pace for 100 miles, it can help us to imagine moving our edge, our comfort zone, out a bit farther than we what we thought was possible. The amazing achievement of others somehow allows us to dream just a bit bigger.

Live, train and run without limits.

May 23 - A work in progress

How we run, the thoughts we have about running and what completes us as a runner will continue to evolve, adding various layers to this running life that only makes it better. In the early years we enjoy the simple breakthroughs in time and speed. As we get deeper into the run, learning and growing faster from books, magazines, coaches, speed work, schedules, high-mileage and racing, our passion grows. Eventually our running may transition into the social framework of life. Training partners, running clubs, group trips to races and shared running experiences may be what gets us out the door. After years on the road, we become coaches for new runners, guiding them past mistakes and helping them accomplish their personal goals, allowing for us to bask in the glory of their success along with our own. All the long and hard miles will give us insight into something we can share. What an amazing running life--now, and until they throw the dirt on us!

Get out there--enjoy, learn, share, and run.

May 24 - You never know what kind of run you'll get today

I am amazed how the miles fly by when the senses are fueled with the smells, sights and sounds of a country dirt road, a single track trail through the woods or even running down a subdivision street that is waking to a new day. Dang, that about covers most runs. So, why do the miles seem to crawl by some days on these same roads and trails and fly by on others? Why do I keep repeating the important themes?

Don't skip today, it may be the best!

May 25 - The world is watching

If you miss a day of running, nobody knows. If you miss two days or running, YOU know; if you miss 3 in a row, everybody knows! Okay, the reality is that nobody cares about our running and they actually don't know, but in the mind of a runner, it seems like it. That said, you'd better get out the door today or . . .

Everyone will know!

May 26 - For every run, a reason

Today, the meditative and philosophical stream-of-consciousness aspects of the run, in combination with living in the moment, may fulfill us to the core. Some days, we need to run long and alone, on other days, we may enjoy sharing the moment, sharing thoughts or sharing only the sounds of footfalls and labored breath. What wonderful choices we have when making our plans to get out the door.

Run the run you need today.

May 27 - You yourself

When we take ourselves to our own personal physical limits and beyond, only we can judge the accomplishment, only we know the barriers we have broken. Sure, others can see our finish times in events or may even share a breakthrough run side-by-side with us, but on any given day the effort we put forth, regardless of the finish time, can only be measured by us. That said, to be motivated to be our best, we must be our own cheerleaders. What others observe and comment about our running accomplishments can boost the ego but may also bring us down. What counts and will take us to the next level is what we ourselves have witnessed and know is true. Be honest with yourself, be proud of yourself.

Every one of your runs is heroic, especially today's.

May 28 - Enjoy a bit of "still life"

A line I use often is, "Listen to your body, except when you're in a race!" The reality is that when racing and you flirt with your limits and your body will often yell, "Back off!" This inner struggle might go on 'til the finish, and perhaps end with a personal best! (I'm not saying to ignore increasing pain from potential injury, that, you pay attention to!) That said, when it comes to the daily run, your body is your partner and when it throws fatigue and lethargy at you, it's not always a time to push through it. It may be time to take stock and be sure you are not digging a hole that might swallow you. Training is not racing. Listen to the body, perhaps give it a break and take some time to look around at this amazing world in slow motion. Perhaps it' time to enjoy a bit of "still life." Tomorrow, or maybe the day after, your mind and body will be in alignment, ready to put the hammer down again.

Listen to your body, kind of anyway.

May 29 - Run and inspire others

A few years back, I got to witness 92-year-old Harriette Thompson finishing the San Diego Marathon, her 18th marathon, showing the world that our sport is there for everyone and giving us hope for a rich and long road ahead. Get out for a run, get out and inspire others!

Harriette is out there training, we have no excuse.

May 30 - There are no bad runs

Some running days are diamonds, others, not so much. I've run marathons where the miles seemed effortless and the final miles were my fastest. I've also headed out for runs that were a herculean effort from the start, each mile requiring me to use every mental and physical tool in the book to keep from walking, or for that matter, quitting altogether. The fast marathon looks good in the result listing, and the satisfaction of doing a lot of things right and things going right is rewarding. On the flip side, that miserable run I gutted through gave me a good look at what I am made of, who I am and who I might be. I felt more deserving of a medal at the end of that slow, miserable run than at many of the finish lines I've crossed. I'm not saying I hope for more tough runs, but I am saying BRING IT ON! I've been there and know I am ready for the good fight.

Every run is a gift, even the ones that suck.

May 31 - Philosophy of Running

It's always easy to preach to the choir, which as runners, you get. I'm sure there is nothing written in this book that you don't already know, but it's nice to get confirmation of your choices in life, perhaps keeping you on track (or road or trail). I've read that a philosopher is someone who tries to say or put down in words what we all know and think already. I guess that's what I attempt to do when it comes to writing about the daily run, our daily bread. That said, it would have been far-out to discuss running in the public baths with Plato or Aristotle in ancient Greece where running was hip and they dreamed up the Olympics and painted naked runners on red clay pots!

Give us this day our daily run, and we'll get through the rest.

June

June 1 - Life, it's all or nothing

When looking at the daily calendar and to-do lists, we're reminded that life is busy, complicated and at times overwhelming. And to think--we *choose* to live like this! The other option is to do nothing, an option which comes with the stress of boredom, laziness and feelings of failure. There really is no in-between or moderation; once you take on responsibility, be ready to rock and roll. What's this got to do with running? I'm sure you already know, you're a runner--I've just described your MO! As we crunch the daily run into the schedule, the magic happens. Somehow this busy life is fulfilling and gives us the best life. Bring it on! Busy people do everything, the rest do . . . not much.

Do everything, today!

June 2 - Plan to enter a race, then make it happen

Runners are creatures of habit; it goes with the territory. Consistency comes from having a plan. Nobody has the time to sneak in a run in this busy life, and as I've said, it must be part of the schedule. Spontaneity is icing on the cake, but it can't be our daily bread. This same mindset works into the event side of our running. Runners are good at maintaining traditions. Many of us have a list of certain events we run year after year, we know where to park, what to expect and can compare our fitness level over the years knowing the course and when we've done well, making it a much more rewarding experience. That said, if your running is inconsistent, get out your daily planner and make a commitment to your runs, making them as much of a priority as the so-called important stuff. What event are you training for? If you have no answer, it's time to sign up for one. Goals will get you out the door. Which event? Ask friends, read reviews, start with established events with a rich history that you will be woven into.

Run today and plan for tomorrow's run when you are done.

June 3 - National Running Day

For us who have been lucky enough to embrace running as a lifestyle, every day is National Running Day. But for the rest of the world, it's the first

Wednesday in June. When I hear John Lennon's song, *Imagine*, I can't help but imagine a world where everyone is a runner. Maybe someday they'll join us, and the world will run as one. For now, let's get out there and set the example, better yet, invite a non-runner out for a walk/run and share the gift on this holiday.

Get out and celebrate today with a run with the world!

June 4 - They say patience is a virtue

I'm sure many of you are type As who have a hard time with the speed limit, saying no to anything and not doing everything to excess; yet, we are attracted to a sport where patience is required at every turn. Patience is needed while slowly building up our weekly mileage, while tapering for a race, while recovering from a race, while holding back the pace during the beginning of a race, while dealing with injuries and the list goes on. No real point here, just an observation, AS I PATIENTLY RECOVER FROM MY MARATHON, NOT RUNNING HARD OR LONG FOR A FEW WEEKS, AND TRYING NOT TO THROW OR BREAK STUFF!

Get out and run if you can and should.

June 5 - The fire burns

Aging up, slowing down . . . so what? If you're working hard and you're at your edge, that's all that matters. Don't let ego get in the way of the personal satisfaction of laying it all on the line and giving it your best. I'm running a few minutes per mile slower than my fastest years, but the fire burns and the effort and feelings experienced while running and racing are as fulfilling as ever. This also relates to coming back from injury or time away from running. Where you're at today is all that matters, so get out there and give it all you have.

Savor the old burn.

June 6 - Diamond days, precious days

Twenty-five years ago, after setting PRs for just about every running and triathlon distance, my aortic heart valve stuck open, sending me into congestive heart failure. Holy crap. This problem came up from and undetected birth defect of the valve. I had major reconstructive heart surgery, including some human transplant tissue, followed by some serious down time but eventually worked my way back to marathon shape. From the dark days I gained a greater appreciation of the diamond days, days like today! It's time to shut this book and head to the woods to hammer!

Let's do what we can do, now!

June 7 - Let's shake it up

Runners are creatures of habit, often running the same routes at the same time at the same pace, some of us wondering why we don't get faster, duh! To get faster we may have to throw in surges, increase our mileage, play with our pace and perhaps change our form. Are we running on the same flat or wimpy rolling course most of our runs? It's time for us amp it up and find routes filled with long killer hills; better yet, some stump-jumping trails with switchbacks and butt-slide grades that will give us strength and increased range of motion. Tricky footing will help develop ancillary muscles that will help keep us injury-free and will be our go-to/change-up muscles late in the race or run when all others are failing. Let's get out the door and start hammering! All that said, none of this is important as just getting out the door but it can't hurt to shake it up a bit, just sayin'.

Run different today!

June 8 - Pain, it's what we came for

I recently had a COVID-19 test and I found the pain interesting--kind of a cold, hot, quick pain, unlike anything I've felt before. I'd kind of like to have it done again to pay more attention to the sensations. It's a strange thought that as runners, we are used to pain and we run long almost searching for it. It's kind of a game, seeing if we can continue running forward and hold our pace as we go through what is often called the pain cave. We savor the soreness of a hard workout, knowing we've pushed ourselves and have something to show for it. The pain proves that we did the work necessary to move our fitness level forward. Running continues to amaze me. It obviously prepares us for so much in life, even a simple test. By the way, the results came back negative and in only 36 hours.

Get out there and live life in full color, while being smart and safe.

June 9 - Run, run, volunteer, run

It's estimated that only 5 percent of runners who enter races have ever volunteered to work an event. I don't think it's because runners are not generous, but there is a lack of knowledge about signing up to volunteer and what it might entail. It's like entering your first race--the first time you sign up it is a huge step into the unknown, but once you do it you're hooked. Being part of a race crew, playing a part of putting on a successful event and helping other runners reach their goals can be as rewarding as competing. Volunteer this year and I promise you will feel more deserving of your daily run. Look for a volunteer tab or link on the event entry web page on a date that works.

To give is to receive, to run is divine.

June 10 - The run is like a filter

Running seems to melt away anger, frustration and anxiety, bringing the mind back in sync with the body. When we head out the door, all that seems to matter is moving, sweating and grooving into a fluid and efficient rhythm where we become one with our run. The run is like a filter that removes all that drags us down and leaves us clean and clear. We finish with renewed energy, energy that had been mired down by this complicated life.

Be one with the run.

June 11 - Don't take the joy of running for granted

By just knowing you are reading this, I can assume you are living a fitness lifestyle or are at least working toward living one. Either way, you have, or had, the courage to start. You made the hard first steps toward becoming a lifelong athlete and are reaping the physical and psychological rewards that come with it. Bravo! I recently met up with an old high school friend who could not keep up with our weekend warrior activities--fun physical stuff we can do without effort. He was disgusted with himself and the years he has neglected his body. The pain and frustration on his face and in his angry comments to himself made me realize how fortunate we are to be on the right path. To run for the pure joy of running and the satisfaction we get (or are beginning to get) from sweat and sore muscles is the fun part of our daily lives, not a chore, punishment or some dreaded necessary fitness routine, but the highlight of our amazing lives.

You are amazing, and will continue to be if you get out that door!

June 12 - Run, and remember this is what we do for fun!

Are you taking your running too seriously? Are you following a schedule that runs your life? This is a common feeling, especially when training for a marathon or half. Yes, when training for a long-term goal it takes dedication, and running must move up on the list of priorities, but some things in life are too cool to miss! It helps me to remember training is more art than science and that if you look at 10 different training schedules you will see huge differences. All the schedules can get you to the goal, so the moral of the story is you can adjust the plan! You can split long runs into two runs on the same day, you can skip a long run to run a race, you can taper for a marathon 4 weeks, 3 weeks, 2 weeks or one week, got the picture? Lighten up, live it up, say yes to invitations to do cool stuff with friends, and adjust! All that said, the longer this sport is part of our lives, the coolest stuff that comes up has running involved!

Get in all life has to offer, make sure it includes today's run!

June 13 - Run, live, smile, die

The next time someone tells you that running might not make you live longer, just tell them, "That's okay, I'm just hoping for some compression of morbidity," then they will then slink off to Google it. The theory, states: would you rather be living it up and running every day until you are 88 and then just drop dead? Or would you rather live a sedentary life, develop congestive heart failure at 75, spend 15 years in a nursing home with multiple disease factors due to lifestyle with no quality of life, then die at 90?

Get out the door and compress that dang morbidity.

June 14 - Put some dirt underfoot

If you don't already, add some trails to your runs. Running the uneven surface works your core and develops the ancillary muscles of the leg and foot, creating more of a muscular balance than the narrow range of muscular use from running on pavement. This variety reduces the chance of overuse injuries and will give you some go-to muscles for late in a long run or race. Another plus, once back on the road, you will run faster with less perceived effort. The value of getting out of the man-made world, away from road noise and dirty air make trail-running a great choice.

Get on a trail and get in a valuable run, today!

June 15 - Run smart, run healthy

As runners, we drink a lot more fluid and consume more calories than those who are sedentary. That said, our risk of health problems due to taking in chemicals, pharmaceuticals and other impurities in our food and water may also be greater. In addition, we suck in a lot more air that is filtered by our lungs than the average couch potato. I believe we need to keep this in mind and look to run away from busy roadways and dirty air and look for sources of healthy food and pure water. We need to be aware.

Run smart, live smart, today.

June 16 - When the run is going well, keep on going!

There is no better time to get in a long run than to start it at the end of the running distance you had planned for the day. Perhaps reset your watch and start fresh--you can't beat a bonus run! Resetting the watch is just a little mental trick, it's not like we don't know we just put in an awesome run. Getting home to write a big number in the log when we didn't expect it can sure supercharge our running week! We are so lucky to be able to run away from our troubles, guilt-free, especially troubles like stress, obesity, heart disease, arthritis, Alzheimer's and bad guys.

Run short and long, today!

June 17 - We really are only as strong as our weakest link, dang

Avoiding injury by having good core strength and flexibility is key, but who has the time? And if you're like I was, only enjoying the aerobic part of fitness, making the time for it was harder yet. I used to joke that because I am a runner, I never have to exercise, as if running gave me a free pass. The reality is this is only partly true. Yes, I don't consider running exercise, it is my passion, the highlight of my day, but alas, I need a core workout also or would risk painful time away from my runs. The answer was to find a non-aerobic passion that fit the bill, and yoga was my answer. Like running, I did not magically do yoga once and become hooked, it was a slow, frustrating process. Like running, I had to stick with yoga long enough to experience positive results that motivated me. After months of yoga, I finally noticed improved muscle tone and flexibility, but most importantly, I developed a natural high, what I call, my yoga buzz. I go to a yoga class once in a while but the majority of my sessions are alone, either with online yoga or just doing poses that I've learned and work for me, making it as convenient as my run. May you find a non-aerobic, core passion, so you can run forever, with no exercise involved!

In the meantime, go run!

June 18 - Peter Pan had it right

Running is a playful, childlike activity, an escape from what would be considered appropriate adult behavior. I find that when I lock my office door, strip out of the work clothes and into my running "play" clothes for a lunchtime run, I feel like Peter Pan. I dash out through the parking lot and smile as I start to groove on down the road into the rhythm of the run, unplugged and free. I soon forget about all the stuff that seemed so pressing and suffocating. After a few miles I return a far more awake and productive worker than when I left, ripping through the to-do list at PR pace.

Never ever get old, never ever miss your run.

June 19 - Pre-race jitters, YIKES!

YIKES! It's the feeling I get when race day draws near for every race, no matter how important or insignificant the event is to me. Even after all these years, the nervous jitters attack! The reality is that our race, our run, is personal; we are the only one who cares about the outcome. No, the world is not watching and no one else really cares. Our training is done or not done, we are either healthy or on the mend with hope and our strategy is pretty much set, so being nervous is unproductive stress. I find that reminding myself of the reality of the situation reduces my race anxiety from YIKES! to yikes. Maybe reading this will do the same for you.

Just run . . . yikes.

June 20 - We could do this naked

Part of our love of running comes from the no-nonsense simplicity and convenience of the sport, with no complicated or expensive equipment. And it takes place right out our front door. I'm sure many of us feel like we are prisoners to a life that demands us constantly to learn new technologies and to keep pace with the competition. The run allows us to unplug, reboot and shut down all the life-sucking applications running in the background. Running--as simple as it gets.

Let's get out for a run, then press, restart.

June 21 - Look forward to right now

While out on a run I too often think of the run as a training run with my thoughts directed to an upcoming event, even when the event is months away. Long-term goals add to the richness of this running life, but I realized I needed to remind myself to not lose sight of the moment, which can short-change every precious day. Over the past year, I've made it a point to ask myself what I would notice on my run if I knew this run would be my last. This has now become a habit, like starting my watch, and I believe it has added something I was missing to my daily life and especially to my daily run. The sun on my face, the air going over my skin, my breathing, the feel of the earth under foot and how my body reacts and flows are some common thoughts. I observe every little thing from architecture to landscape. I always notice the look of the sky, and the weather. For sure, the elements have become an important part of the experience to be savored, no matter what the conditions--days I would have looked at as miserable now add spice and texture to my run. Once I've captured the moment, my mind may still drift off to another place, but in a seemingly better context than where it might have been in the past.

Run in the moment.

June 22 - Running will always take you back

We all take breaks from running from time to time, be it from a physical issue or some other complication in life. A common theme is, "I used to be a runner, but it somehow slipped away from me." The good news is that running is always there waiting for you when you decide to return. Yes, running will punish you a bit for the break as you work yourself back into some semblance of shape, but it will also reward you for your effort each and every time you get out the door. That said, we all know that when we stay consistent with our running, the positive physical and psychological aspects we get from our daily run are accentuated to a level above the astral plane. The daily investment in running is a fine return, but consistency is like compound interest, the more you run, the greater the reward.

Thank today's run for always being there for you.

June 23 - Man is harder than iron, stronger than stone and more fragile than a rose

I'm guessing this line came from an injured runner. It's amazing how we can train the body to run great one season, then the next season we have some nagging pain that won't let us finish a mile, dang. One day we might get out of a car or out of bed the wrong way and break a leg or have some similar freak injury. One thing is certain, life is not fair. For sure, we'd rather get a running injury from being bull-headed and doing something dumb than have our body fail while training smart, but stuff happens. When it does, we do what has to be done to get back to what we love and live for. At the time life craps on us, it's hard to accept the fact that adversity and how we get through it makes us who we are and leaves us better equipped to take on all this life can throw at us, eventually adding to our greatness. It takes a long time to make a diamond!

Run, fall, break, and come back stronger.

June 24 - The Obsessed Runner explains

When I say I am an admitted obsessed runner, it doesn't necessarily mean I run more than others I know, or as fast. Actually, because of my passion for everything running, I may actually be a bit conservative with my personal running, knowing that overuse injuries can stop me from my daily run, a painful reality I have learned over my 40 years as a runner. I also make family a priority ahead of my running, knowing that my life without them would be a life without joy, including my running life. So yes, almost every aspect of my daily life, including most thoughts and dreams, make me an admitted obsessed runner.

Respect the culture, respect your passion, and run today, so you can run forever.

June 25 - Don't always listen to your body

When the run is going well and your body wants to go, pass up the house and keep going! Don't get hung up on your schedule or the distance you had planned to run; take advantage. When the run sucks and you have tried every trick in your arsenal and can't talk the body into one more step, head for home and try again tomorrow. The moral of this story is to listen to your body during training runs, but not without an argument. That said, never listen to your body during a race, especially a long race. At some point, it will get pissed off. Yes, listen to it when talking about specific pain, but not when it gets bitchy about misery and fatigue.

Run where the run takes you.

June 26 - Run today because you can

As runners, we learn the body is as strong as it is fragile. It can be trained and conditioned to run 26 miles and it can shrivel up and die from an invisible germ or cancer. The body is complicated, the body is amazing, life is complicated, life is amazing. Enjoy every healthy day and never take it for granted. Get out and run and enjoy. Knowing how good it was and how good it can be gives us the strength to crawl and fight our way back when the dark days hit. Yes, I repeat the important stuff but I try to change up the words so you continue to pay attention!

Today's run is tomorrows cure.

June 27 - Gold medal memories

For those of us who have been at the running game for many years, our best times may be behind us, but perhaps not our best or most memorable runs. In 2010 I ran Boston with my wife and son, a weekend that lives on in memory as a highlight of my running life, even though I fell apart and finished far behind them. All runs are not created equal--our fitness level, our mental and physical health, the weather, family, financial and career problems all come into play. Some of our most difficult runs, with our slowest times ever, when we have overcome so much just to finish, can live on as some of our greatest accomplishments.

Some runs, like the one with my family, are cherished not because of my run because of our time together.

This run may change everything, don't miss it.

June 28 - We learn all we need from running

When we hit the finish line, we get to reap the rewards from our long-term goal planning and execution. Training for an event teaches us the life skills that will help bring us success in all aspects of this busy and wonderful life. For those of us who have been at this a while, each event is a bit of a refresher course in time management and planning. We find that during the time period that we train for a specific race, our life's direction seems clear and focused and our productivity is high in all areas. When not in training we can get sidetracked with nonsense. Perhaps the answer is to always have a running goal.

Plan, run, learn, race, but train today!

June 29 - Read and run

Motivational running books and magazines can help get us out the door. The trick is to leave them lying around all over the house, in your car and at work. When waffling on getting out the door, pick one up and after a few pages, the excitement, or guilt, will set in and you will soon be in the training mindset. Motivational movies can do the same, but you might get caught up and find yourself headed out for a middle of the night run!

Read short, run long.

June 30 - Stay calm and run on

We run for a lot of reasons, for many of us, one reason is to escape the stress of our busy lives. That said, our running should never be a cause of stress, If it is, it's time to step back and assess the reason and work it out before our next run. No matter how slow, how fast or how far off we land from our running goals, we must keep in mind that this is how we spend our leisure time, the most precious hours of our day. As my wise friend John A. always says, "If it's not fun, don't do it!" Each healthy day we can get out for a run is a gift. The world news is a reminder of how fortunate most of us are. While so many are dealing with famine, war, terrorism, genocide and diseases like Leukemia, here we are, worrying about missing out on an age group award, a Boston qualifying time or getting in our minimum number of steps, miles or whatever on our fitness app, duh. The news should be a daily reminder for us to appreciate every run and even if the run sucks, or we don't hit the planned distance or whatever, we should find a smile to share with the world!

Stay calm, run and smile today.

July

July 1 - This running life is "simply" the best!

I spent a Summer weekend at a nonrunning friend's cottage that included jet skis, ATV's, gas cans and dragging around big trailers, followed by lots of sitting around. It was a weekend where I had to sneak in the run. My next Summer weekend was at a cottage with running friends that included morning and evening runs, walks on the beach and a special day starting with a social 3-mile run to town for the blueberry festival 5K followed by the 3-mile run home while discussing the world. This part was similar to when we sat around the previous weekend, without the sitting. Oh yeah, both weekends included fine wine and both were fun times with great friends. The moral of the story? Enjoy this rich and varied life and if necessary, sneak in a run to do this.

Get out and train for the weekend.

July 2 - I hate running!

Recently, I've come across two tongue-in-cheek articles by passionate runners, explaining how they hate running. Cute lines like, "I even have 3 pairs of my favorite running shoes that I hate to run in." and, "I usually hate running 5 days a week but shoot for 6." Both articles ended the same, explaining that the worst thing about running is the fear that one day, running might not be an option, and how would they go on. The love/hate relationship is hard to explain, but love songs like, *I Love You so Much It Hurts*, by Floyd Tillman, resonate with us all. The most difficult things in life give us so much in return, we learn who we are and who we might be. The fact that nothing good comes easy is a reality and yes, we only truly appreciate the things we work for.

Let's get out and hurt so good.

July 3 - Hero worship

I ran into my American hero last week, Bob, pounding out the miles at Island Lake Recreation Area. Bob is over 80 years young, a great dad, husband, marathon runner, IRONMAN® triathlete and for as long as I've known him, a sober alcoholic, a man who traded up in the obsession game! Bob worked into his 70s so he could afford the toys of his trade, running shoes, fast bikes, wetsuits and race entry fees. Thanks for showing us the way, Bob.

Bob set the bar, let's go for it.

July 4 - The shape of America

Those of us who live the running life may have a skewed view of the average American when it comes to fitness. For me, being in the running and event business only adds to my warped view. Sure, day to day life brings us in contact with plenty of people in horrible shape, including some of our own friends and family, but overall, I'd guess we still get a false sense of the true shape of this country. It struck me this week while observing the crowd along a northern Michigan holiday parade route. Yikes! The number of "large" people (I'm sure there is a politically correct word) and the number of people who still smoke was a bit of a shock. Perhaps it's always been this way and I am a poor observer, but my gut feel is that the country is on a downward slide. Not that I have the answers; but getting out there and setting the example, talking positively with people about running and taking the time to get a non-fit neighbor out for an easy run or walk would be a start.

Get out and run, get out and be an example.

July 5 - Light a fire

Today I was the speaker for a lunch series on fitness at a local corporation. I was reminded that when people give running a try, as one woman put it, "It just sucks." It struck me that the truth is, when we try a new physical activity that our bodies and minds don't have a feel for, this makes sense. Nothing good comes easy, especially in running. The benefits come slow but continue to grow as we stick with it. Personal records, increased self-esteem and the pure joy of the effortless runs can't be experienced without putting in some hard time at the beginning. For sure, this needs to be stressed to the new runner. I think minimally, we should ask them to commit to 3 days a week for 4 weeks while keeping a log that tracks pace, distance and weekly total. This might get them over the first hurdle. The motivational thought of knowing they have a 4-week streak of runs that will end if they give it up might be just what they need to keep the fragile little flame lit long enough to get to the blazes of personal glory.

Help someone start a fire, or get your fire started today.

July 6 - Your consistency could save your life

As runners, we are far more aware of our health status than the average American; we are in touch with our bodies because we ask a lot of them daily and can tell when things are even a bit out of whack. I continually talk to runners who have learned about serious health issues in their early stages because of this awareness, certainly an advantage to get things back on the right track, perhaps saving their life. The same insight makes runners good patients, we will do what it takes to recover and get back out there. This is true for our diets too. As runners, we find out what foods work for us, which are usually pretty healthy. We naturally avoid high-fat meals that don't allow us to get out for a run, either from sluggishness or digestive issues. Running, the sport that keeps on giving, as long as you keep getting out the door.

So, get out the door!

July 7 - Be proud of what you do

It seems I'm surrounded by more athletes who are faster, do harder workouts and run more mileage than ever before. As silly as it may sound, I still find myself feeling a bit embarrassed when asked what kind of mileage I'm running or what kind of time I hope to run in an upcoming race, wondering how I compare. On the other hand, I cringe when I hear someone say, I'm not really a runner, I only run 3 or 4 miles 3 or 4 times a week. I let them know that they certainly are runners and that consistently running 10 miles per week or more is a serious commitment to the sport. Our perception may be our reality, but it's a reality we can change by changing our perception, so let's! Please slap me the next time I get embarrassed when talking about my running; I'll do the same for you!

We are all running rock stars!

July 8 - This is not a dress rehearsal

I am a fan of the line: "This is not a dress rehearsal." Every day is precious, as I was reminded this year when I lost two young friends to sudden illness and death. Yes, we may be training for a goal event, saving money for some future purchase or working on some elaborate long-term project. But this stuff all depends on what tomorrow brings. We know it's important to take time each day and live in the moment. It takes effort, but the effort is always rewarded. Our run fits this live-in-the-moment requirement pretty well. That said, no matter how passionate we are about our daily run, it still takes an effort to leave all those projects behind and get ourselves out the door each day. When we finish our run, we realize how important the run was to our lives and we are always happy we ran. So why in the heck don't we have that same feeling and realization as we contemplate getting out for our run? This continues to baffle me, but it is what it is.

Get out and run, like you always will.

July 9 - Two pair beats one of a kind

Why is it so hard to head out for a run in the rain but such a fun and free felling when we are out running and get caught in the rain? I headed out today in a fresh and flashy pair of Brooks running shoes for a few dirt road miles and down came the rain, giving my new kicks a well-worn look, dang. On a different note, the shoes performed wonderfully, I hope it's the beginning of a long-term love affair. I'm sure my old pair of Asics are in a jealous rage. It's not easy to find shoes that work well and we love, even harder to find a different brand and model to alternate when running the roads, but by varying the shoes, we reduce the chance of overuse injuries that are accentuated when the foot strike is the same over and over.

Take one of those pairs out on a hot date today!

July 10 - It is a good morning!

"Good morning" is a greeting so automatic, but somehow it always rings true, often coming from a passing stranger on the morning run. Every day we can get out is a gift and every day and every running route has something unique to offer. From the excitement, danger and challenge we get from extreme weather days to the rave-run, perfect-temperature days that can only be appreciated by experiencing the wicked ones. The daily struggle to wake early and get out the door is always rewarded. Seek and ye shall find. Without the run it is difficult to clear the morning haze, a blah that can leave us in a funk that can last all day and blur one day into the next . . . until we finally run out the door again. Yikes!

It is a good morning, don't miss it.

July 11 - Sleep running

For many of us, our bodies like to go for a run about two hours after we wake up. This works out fine on the day of an event but on a normal day with the time constraints of life, we go through the usual torture, head games and trickery to get up and drag ourselves out the door just minutes after waking. A few miles into the run, it is not uncommon to wake up and be startled to find where we are and instantly feel wonderfully alive, making the torture of getting out the door worthwhile. Knowing this and going through the same scenario day after day you'd think we would just skip the drama and run out the door. The same goes for the evening run; we may get home brain-dead and tired and it amazes us how going out for a run slaps us awake and leaves us exhilarated, content and ready to rock the night.

Running is truly a miracle drug. Get out and get your fix.

July 12 - Some days are diamonds, some days are stone

As I've said many times, enjoy every healthy running day, because we are not as bulletproof as we'd like, and we are only as strong as the weakest link. It seems that the silliest little issues--pain, head cold, stomach issues or whatever, can derail our carefully designed training plan and crush the dream of an upcoming race, or the most valuable thing of all, our daily run. Dang! Be realistic; setbacks are part of who we are. How we come back and how we handle adversity are the true grit of training, jumping from the training plan to the recovery plan. Yes, I repeat the . . .

Put your chin up when get knocked down, it's part of the gig.

July 13 - Run away from politics

The ability to endure, which we learn from our running life, may not seem helpful when it comes to seemingly endless election years. But running gives us a place to sort out the world. It gives us time alone, away from the media, the pundits and the rhetoric, a time to clear our heads enjoy the simple freedoms we have in this amazing county, perhaps renewing our hope. The run is rarely pessimistic.

May today's run give you peace.

July 14 - You may not live to be 100

One day I returned home after a long hard run and was sitting on the back porch in a sweaty post-run haze. My dad looked at me shaking his head and commented, "You might not live to be 100 . . . but it will sure seem like it." My dad was from an old-world family and my running passion took a while for him to accept. Later in life, he let me know that he was proud of his running son and that he could see that it was a positive influence, giving me a discipline and consistency that carried over to my work and family life. I've come to realize my running is much like the influence my dad worked to give me growing up. Running kind of picks up from where our parents or mentors left off. I lost my dad recently, and never have my runs been such a valuable comfort to me. I've been spending the miles recalling our times together, hearing his voice, his laugh and seeing his smile.

You never really run alone, dedicate your run today.

July 15 - Be careful out there, heat kills

Diggin' the heat! As you know, I love extremes, they are truly the spice of life. Give me a humid 95-degree or a 10-below-zero 3-mile run and I'll trade them for any blah 10-mile run on a so-called nice day. A short run in extreme conditions is such great bang for the buck, an efficient use of time that leaves us not only wasted, but fulfilled, raising our self-esteem and that darn feeling of smug satisfaction we get over the rest of the world that stays inside re-breathing stale heated or cooled air. All that said, running in the heat is the most dangerous condition you will face as a runner. Heat kills, so take a run in the heat seriously. Run short, run in shade, run hydrated by more than just water and ideally, finish where you can jump in a lake or stand under a cold hose. Stop and walk if you feel strange.

Run smart, but don't miss the adventure.

July 16 - It's deja vu all over again

Every running "first" is welded into our minds in detail, like the first time we consciously set out to go for a run, the first running event we entered, or the first time we ran or raced farther ever before. I find these first-time memories popping up from time to time, usually while on the run when some feeling, sight or whatever takes me back. I was giving this some conscious thought on the run yesterday while laying out a course for a local 5K. I knew there would be many running their first 5K and I was thinking how the course would look and be remembered by them--the pre-race nerves, the surface of the road, the weather, the look of the neighborhood, etc. Doing this brought a flood of running memories, a cathartic feeling not quite explainable. It struck me that each run we go on connects us to every run we've ever been on and even future runs we have planned. They are connected both physically through the training effect and mentally with our thoughts and feelings. Dang this is a cool sport!

May today's run be a magical mystery trip to runs past and future!

July 17 - Never give up

We strive for the complete fitness lifestyle, eating healthy, getting in the scheduled runs, workouts, core work, sleep, and getting in the personal best shape of our lives. In reality, there are far too many days with work and family issues that get out of control, leaving us with no time for the workout. We may find ourselves skipping meals or sleep, and worse yet, we may follow it up with an overindulgent night out that we trick ourselves into thinking we deserve for stress reduction or other nonsense. But we know the reality is a deeper hole. Fitness, like freedom and everything precious, takes constant vigilance and hard work. It is a lifelong battle with victories and setbacks but always worth every ounce of energy we put forth. Never ever give up, each hard-won fitness victory is sweet and worth a lifetime of struggle.

We start again today with a run!

July 18 - Hot runs count double

I admit, I'm obsessed with miles--miles ran today, total miles for the week, for the year, etc. Yes, a pretty flawed obsession when it comes to getting out there for a brutal 3 miles in hot, humid conditions, or a trail run with bad footing and thousands of feet of climbing or running into an endless 20 mile- per-hour headwind. Distance is often the least relevant aspect of a run. But time, distance and speed are all our GPS watches and phone apps track. Okay, feet climbed may be in there but the point is that it's hard to put a number on hard work. We personally know the incredible effort we are putting out to get in these wicked miles, so it's up to us to give ourselves credit. Let's call the effort we put in for a mile on a great route on a great day the baseline. Then, we go in to our Strava account or wherever we keep track and override the numbers without an ounce of guilt! Yep, today's 3 just became 6. Six miles you can be proud of!

Run safe out there and give yourself credit.

July 19 - Hydrate, hydrate, hydrate!

I had a running buddy who refused to drink water or anything on runs less than 10 miles, even on hot days, claiming he was fine without it. It was not that he thought it macho to run without drinking, but he thought it was a hassle carry water or stop for it. The truth is, dehydration can reduce your body's ability to absorb shock to the joints, to the spinal cord and to the brain. Hydration helps deliver oxygen to the body, regulates your temperature, helps maintain your blood pressure and keeps your airways from restricting. (*Fifteen Benefits of Drinking Water*, by James McIntosh, MedicalNewsToday.com, July 16, 2018) The point is that he was wrong, and he could have been a heathier, better runner with proper hydration.

Don't skip today's run and don't skip your water intake!

July 20 - When the run no longer seems fun

It can happen--not all at once--but a feeling sneaks in slowly over time--you decide running is just not fun anymore. You find yourself bored and thinking only of the time you have left to get it over with and other things you would rather be doing in life. I'm guessing this kind of funk happens in all areas of our lives, kind of like a mid-life crisis. For me, I equate it to a minister doubting the existence of God at some point. I have watched other running friends face these demons and how it played out. To turn this monster, runaway-train thought pattern around, it might take hitting rock bottom for some of us to finally throw on the brakes and stop, cold turkey. I believe this gap, or void, might be needed for some of us to see past the negative thoughts and become a born-again runner. Perhaps stopping running for enough time to realize all we have lost might be necessary to re-kindle the flame. Perhaps reading about this scenario might save you the pain. Get out there today and focus on all that is right with your run, the glory of the run, a run you control, perhaps avoiding this negative rabbit hole all together, forever.

Shine a light on your run today.

July 21 - Is our running insane?

It is said that the definition of Insanity is doing the same thing over and over again and expecting different results. This quote, that some attribute to Albert Einstein, can be applied to the way some of us runners train for events, or how we run in general. Many of us are creatures of habit, even if they are bad habits. I use the term "many" because I'm guessing I'm not the only one. I have asked myself, "Why do I run so slow? I am not making changes to my running that might make me fast. I have the habit of running most of my miles at the same pace and often on the same course and am not becoming a faster, better runner, duh. Perhaps it's time to use our daily run as an experiment, planning a mix of pace, hills and distance. We might not only become faster and less injury-prone, but we might light a new fire of excitement. My plan: hammer every other mile tomorrow. My plan for the next day? I'm not sure, but I'm excited to make the plan!

Break out of the rut and run off the dust today.

July 22 - All those who wander are not lost

It's time to plan a long fun Summer vacation run, even if you are not on vacation! Invite along some flexible, open-minded running friends or go it alone. The normal training day does not allow time for a run that includes shopping, a stop at a bar and sight-seeing. In addition, it takes the vacation or lazy weekend mentality to make this run work. Plan this excursion on a warm, Summer day, so stopping and being wet and cold is not an issue. Bring cash and a water carrier with an area to pack treasures and some energy food.

The route can be a big loop or point to point if you have a return strategy. Include points of interest like a roadside stand, waterfall, scenic view spot, or skinny-dipping hole and a shorter route back, with more points of interest like a dive bar, model homes, or garage sales. Do the town, hit the galleries, pubs, hot spots and a running shoe store. Don't be afraid to do some, dare I use the word, walking! Actually, you should throw in a bunch of walking from the start, so pace does not become part of the plan! Enjoy every minute!

Run, sun, sip, walk, and wander--soon!

July 23 - When the run goes bad

Today I was attempting to be an alchemist (Isn't that someone who tries to turn sh-t into gold?). Anyway, I attempted to turn my sh-tty run into something positive. For 10 miles I felt just awful, using both mental and physical energy to turn it around. I lied to myself, restarted my watch a few times and stopped to walk and shake off the demons, all to no avail. Tomorrow's run will be awesome. I'll appreciate it because of today's sh-tty run! Finally, I found something positive about today's run!

Run, scream and wave your arms like a raving lunatic, it can't hurt!

July 24 - Off the wagon

I hope last week's running was better for you than me. I fell off the running wagon a bit and hit my low miles for the year. No good excuses, because there is no such thing when it comes to running. Time to regroup. I'm tapered and ready to crush this week. I started it with a long trail run this morning where I saw deer, wild turkeys and a killer sunrise. I got up at 5 a.m. which I don't do often. For those of you who get up early and stumble out into the dark to get in your miles, I commend you! My only problem is that it's now 9:30 a.m. and I'm ready for lunch!

Stay on the wagon, or get back on it NOW!

July 25 - Dog Days

Just when the schedule is calling for more miles, the dog days seem to want to put a bite in our motivation. If I made the running rules I would have all miles count double from now until the end of August. That said, we all have the ability to make our own rules when it comes to the stuff we do for fun in life. We need to remember to go easy on ourselves. Head for the shade and trails. Hydrate but also pour a bit of water on your skin, drinking does little to bring down the body temperature, but external cooling WORKS. Bring ice along and put under your hat, better yet, near your groin, YIKES!

Run smart, run cool, then jump in a lake.

July 26 - Another hot day to run, sweat and smile

I just finished a Summer trail run where I dealt with heat, humidity, sweat, bugs, dust, long hard climbs, mud, overgrown thorny areas, bad footing, chafe, and fatigue. But I also encountered deer, woodchucks, rabbits, a symphony of beautiful bird songs, a stretch of cool, shady, pine-needle-carpeted trail, wonderfully long, effortless, downhill stretches, several river and lake vistas from the ridges, wildflower meadows and a feeling of total fulfillment as I splashed into the cool waters of a crystal clear lake for my finish line. As usual, when all that is encountered on the run is added up, the sum total is clearly in the positive column!

May you finish today's run in the black.

July 27 - Sweet spot

It's bad enough that half the time we have to talk ourselves into the daily run and getting our butt out the door, only to find that our body often rejects the idea of a run even more than us. Luckily, after a mile or two of burps, farts, gas pains, dead legs and a racing heartbeat, the body usually grooves into the idea and smooths out like a finely tuned Indy car, vroom! At this point our attitude does a 180 and the magic of the daily run is on. Sheesh, you would think we could skip the drama and get right into the sweet spot, but I guess that will never happen.

The run is always worth it, get your motor runnin'.

July 28 - Just you and your run

During the COVID-19 lockdown days I worried about my friends who lived alone but now were seriously alone. Those who were dedicated runners shared a similar take on the lack of in-person human contact. Running had become their closest friend, always there for them, ready to head out and spend quality time. Their social media posts referred to the run as a noun. The run was comforting, entertaining, and always interesting. The run would at times make them smile and at times beat them up but like a friend, always a constant.

Go spend some quality time with your run today.

July 29 - Run ruined by routine

Routine is a two-edged sword, on one side it reduces the stress associated with the unknown and keeps us on the roads we know, allowing for a meditative run and a training experience we understand. On the flip side, we mentally block our spirit of adventure and often end up with a ho hum middle-of-the-road life that leaves us wondering what we missed, a wicked stress of its own, one that can make us feel . . . old. Bilbo Baggins comes to mind. Are you squandering one of the precious days of your life on a run that will not be memorable, a run that keeps you from discovering who you are and who you might be? Or, are you heading out for an adventure, perhaps on a run that you might tell stories about until the end of your days! Yes, it might be awful but it might be great. At least it won't be blah.

Run off on a wild adventure.

July 30 - We need to run

Running is play, escape and meditation, it gets us back to being on the same team as our body. We are reminded that our minds and bodies are one and we will remain incomplete, unproductive and unhealthy if we don't nurture this union. We live in a world that separates us from our bodies, a world that asks us to focus our attention on business, family, relationships, productivity and charity. It is our responsibility to take care of ourselves, create the time and expend the energy on what our body and mind need. We must become selfish for the good of the world. If we are without health and happiness, we are the ones in need, therefore not in a position to give to others or play a positive role in this world.

Today's run may be the most important thing we do.

July 31 - Running, the meaning of life

This morning on a quiet country road, I decided that running may be the meaning of life, or at least a big part of mine. During a great run we truly live in the moment with all senses firing on all cylinders with the smells, sights, feel of the wind and weather licking our face. We savor the physical work, fatigue, success and completion, we feel fully alive and know this is where we belong. Perhaps a second run is in order today!

Run and know the truth.

August

August 1 - Hot, hot, hot

Much of what is fun in life is fast or dangerous, like running in the heat! Sure, it can kill you, like so many things that we do for enjoyment; the alternative is to do nothing! I repeat the important stuff. Respect the heat, carry fluid, hydrate, run short, run easy, and run a course you can bail out on quickly. For example, run smaller loops from where you start. The upside is you get a great workout in a short time and each hot run gets you more adapted to the heat, making you one tough cookie! Another great thing--a well-hydrated body runs smoothly in the heat; all the aches and pains seem to disappear and the chance of injury goes way down because your muscles and tendons are warm and pliable. Jump in a lake or run a cold hose over your head when you finish, you will feel fully alive while the rest of the air-conditioned world lives on in a comatose state of boredom!

Run smart, as usual, run today!

August 2 – Each run is a gift

Some days the run comes to us like a wrapped gift, like an unexpected inheritance from a long-lost relative that makes us smile. Other days, the run is a bloody battle with ourselves, the elements, and seemingly uncontrollable forces of the universe teaming up against us. When we get these runs done, it's not with a smile but a personal pride that runs down to our soul, giving us a glimpse of strength and courage we may not have known we had.

Fight the good fight, you will be rewarded every time.

August 3 - Run alone and connected

I use a running app on my phone and I must admit, it helps motivate me out the door. Today's apps are not only a way to log miles and track totals but a way to interact with other runners. You can follow others and be followed, and there is the chance of getting kudos, even for my short, slow runs or walks, much like getting likes on social media! Okay, exactly like it. You can use these apps on many of the GPS watches, but I like the security of running with my phone. (I do keep the ringer off to run in peace.) On almost every run I encounter something beautiful or interesting enough to snap a photo of to add to my post/log. When my day gets long or stressful, these images can plug me back into an energized moment from my run and clear the funk. And yes, by having the phone you may be the first to come upon an accident scene, dial 911, and save a life.

Run fully connected and peacefully alone.

August 4 - Running traditions bring meaning to life

Our sport's roots go back to the ancient Greek Olympics, plus there are historic races like the 100-plus years of the Boston Marathon. We can agree that running as a sport is not a fad and has an excellent foundation. That said, most of us won't be running in the Olympics and even qualifying for the Boston Marathon may be a stretch, but we each start our own traditions that personally motivate us and add so much to our running lives. The greatest traditions can be local family-friendly races where we can test ourselves each year. Better yet, invite nonrunners in your family to join you for their first 5K and build a tradition. We will all be gone someday but new family traditions can live on.

Start a tradition and become part of the run forever.

August 5 - You are a runner, bravo!

By knowing you are reading this, I can assume you are living a fitness lifestyle, or are at least working toward it. Either way, you had the courage to start. You made the hard first steps toward becoming a lifelong athlete and are reaping the physical and psychological rewards that come with it. Bravo! We are fortunate to be on the right path. We run for the pure joy of running and the satisfaction we get from sweat and sore muscles with fitness as a bonus. The run is the fun part of our day, not a chore, punishment or some dreaded necessary fitness routine. It is the highlight of our amazing lives!

Let us continue to get out that door forever. Forever includes today!

August 6 - Today's run will make tomorrow's easy

During our run, my wife, a nurse practitioner specializing in geriatric medicine, said that the secret to longevity is to just keep moving. She shared an example that once a person starts to use a wheelchair to ease the burden of walking, their chances of never walking again are very good and it goes downhill from there. It seemed to me that running teaches us this at an earlier stage in life--skip the run and the next run will only be tougher.

Never ever stop, including today, tomorrow and forever.

August 7 - The run will take you back, promise

My Daughter Anna jumping in here today to get your butt out the door!

There will ALWAYS be an excuse to not get out the door. For me, the last few months brought strep throat, some minor injuries and long weeks at work. My training suffered and after a few weeks of slump, the excuses turned to FEAR! I was afraid that when I finally put the shoes back on and got out there, the run wouldn't take me back. I eventually sucked it up, laced up, grabbed some girlfriends and got out there. Not only did the run take me back, but it gifted me with a rave run. They haven't all been that great, but I'm back out the door and the fear is gone!

Don't be afraid that the run won't be there for you.

August 8 - More thoughts on Peter Pan, my hero

Like Peter Pan says, "Never, never, ever, ever grow up." The running life sure helps keep us acting like kids and fitness in general helps ward off the lethargy of old age. I recently went to a Jack Johnson concert and last night saw Sheryl Crow. The audience for Jack Johnson was significantly younger than the Sheryl Crow crowd. They stood dancing, singing and smiling the entire concert even though Jack Johnson's music was calm and quiet. On the flip side, the Sheryl Crow crowd sat like they were at home watching TV even though the music was rockin'. They were offended anytime someone got up to dance. We can't let this happen to us! Get out and run, get up and dance! Never trust a thought you have while sitting down and never, never, ever, ever, grow up and be a grumpy old, don't-step-on-my-grass kind of person, or ever stop running!

Run so you can, like Peter Pan.

August 9 - No longer running

My day job is putting on races with RF Events. We send reminder emails about upcoming events to our past participants and like any list, we get some opt-outs each week. Most check the box, "I get too many emails." When they give a reason for opting out, it is often, "I no longer run." This answer breaks my heart because I can't even respond to them because their email is no longer available to me, dang. I worry about the reasons—do the emails make them feel guilty or lazy? Did they suffer an injury that will keep them from ever running again? This is a complicated world with real life-and-death situations that can force running to take a back seat. That said, the run is always there to come back to; it is a patient sport that will wait until the day we return. Whatever the reason you are sidelined from the run, consider staying on the running lists. You never know what the future may bring or what might re-light the flame.

Don't opt out of today's run!

August 10 - You have chosen the best sport

When you consider convenience, equipment, financial commitment and exacting motivational results, compared to other sports, running wins, hands down. Besides simplicity, with our sport, the winner is clear. Time, distance and speed rock, they are nonjudgmental, nonpolitical and come with no BS. The clock is honest. When you compare running to a sport like ice dancing where you have to rely on a group of judges giving scores on how it "seemed" to them, you know you have chosen well.

Lace em' up and when you hear the gun, give it your all.

August 11 - When planning a trip, keep running in mind

As I write this I'm staying with my family in a cabin on the island of Dominica with no electricity, invigorating cold showers and more natural beauty than I can describe. Each day starts with a long mountain run, a jump in the ocean followed by a breakfast consisting of local fruit and honey on some killer biscuit from a tin shack bakery. After a long swim I fall asleep reading a book in the shade. Dinner in the local village is always a new kind of fish with several unfamiliar starchy vegetables served on a plywood table where we eat with are hands. The moral of the story? Jump out of the rut, do whatever it takes and spend some quality downtime in a great place to run. Then you can return fit, clear-headed and ready to crank!

Run, plan and live, this is not dress rehearsal.

August 12 - Lie to yourself

When the body just does not want to run today, it's time to lie to it. Promise your body that all you have in mind is a 10-minute jog and that after that, if it still wants to go home and lay on the couch, you will let it. Actually you aren't lying because once you have gone through the trouble of getting on the running gear and start heading up the street, 10 minutes will pass, your energy level will rise and your body will be all in. After the run you will be saying to yourself, "I feel great, what a great run, I'm sure glad we got out the door." It's strange how many times we might have to go through this same scenario and how our bodies can't seem to remember how great we will feel once we are actually running, even though it happens every time. It's just weird, like talking to yourself is weird. As usual, get out that door and the run is licked.

Liar, liar, run like your pants are on fire!

August 13 - The love/hate relationship with a GPS watch

I love and hate my GPS watch, just like any good coach I suppose. I sure miss logging my miles using a fudge factor to tally them. I used to think, okay, a 45-minute run, it felt like 9-minute pace so 5 miles sounds about right today. Now, on a windy day with some bad footing I see I've run 45 minutes, thinking it is a 9-minute pace effort, only to see on my app it's hardly a 10-minute pace and I have at least 5 minutes more to get in my planned 3 miles. Whoever guessed it would take technology to make me honest? I sure miss the days when running for a longer time meant logging more miles! That said, the GPS watch does its job, use one.

If you set up your watch right, it would beep now and tell you to go run!

August 14 - Still diggin' the run after all these years

I must admit, I'm about as obsessed with running now as I have ever been. Several decades of this and I'm still wallowing in it like a pig in mud. This sport is truly a gift. There are lots of ups and downs, but when it's clicking along, life gets no better. Last week I ran my fastest 10K in 8 years. Last night I ran some Rambo-like muddy trails with some stupid steep hills. Tonight, I just finished a killer 9-mile run with my son who is a kick-butt fast runner! Enjoy every day of this running curse and stay over on the dark side till the end. May it never end, and if it does, we will know we left nothing on the table.

Run forever.

August 15 - Stay the course

Few things are as consistent and calming as the daily run in this inconsistent world. The housing and stock market boomed and we ran, the housing market and stock market crashed and we ran, the country continues to go to war and we continue to run. During our runs we have the option to contemplate solutions to the world's problems or to escape reality and enjoy playtime and answer the deep questions, like what shoes to run in or what route to head out on. Either way, we finish energized, focused and ready to take on the day!

I'm out of here, Join me!

August 16 - Run the reality, not what you had planned

As runners we often get hung up with the training schedules, mileage charts, calorie intake, and all sorts of other numbers as we prepare for a big event. Once off-schedule due to injury, family crisis or whatever, we can get discouraged or depressed as we try to get back on. Cramming for the exam is not the answer! The reality is, once off-schedule, the schedule becomes obsolete. Trash it and write a new one based on the time you have now. The only important aspect of this new schedule is that you have confidence in it.

Yes, you can finish the event with far fewer miles or different finish time than you had planned, but keep in mind what's really important. Believe in your schedule and it will work! Use what you know. No more fretting; this is the new reality. Now you can work hard and enjoy training that is fulfilling and fun again!

Don't stress about it, the mission is still on.

August 17 - Weekends are not the only time for the long run

When I can, I love to get the Summer long runs out of the way during the midweek, as weekends tend to be busy. There is something empowering about a stupidly early weekday long run, after which I go through the day feeling mellow and on top of the world. I try not to walk around with that smug feeling of satisfaction showing . . . but I fail at it all the time.

Get in an early long run and smile all day.

August 18 - You are not a slow runner

The pace you run is based somewhat on your training, but most importantly, your body and its history. We may have asthma, diabetes, migraines, Crohn's disease, joint replacements, flat feet, or arthritis. We may have healed broken bones and scar tissue from past surgeries, and we are all different genetically. The point is we are not slow, our pace is unique to all that makes us who we are today. A 12-minute pace may be a world-class effort. What is important is to know the work we did to accomplish our run times and to be proud of the work and the accomplishment.

Run like only you can, today!

August 19 - A year of holes

I broke a toe in April and by cutting a hole in all my running shoes, I was able to run pretty much pain-free during the 5 months it took until I could finally put on a shoe without a hole--just in time for a trip to Barbados, where I ended up with a blister after some long hot runs. Taking a serrated steak knife, again I cut a round hole in the heel of my running shoe just a bit bigger than the blister. I headed out the door pain-free and healing quickly! I felt no effect on the shoes' performance; perhaps I'll cut a few more holes and lighten them up. For your next foot problem, consider going under the knife!

No excuses--get creative, get out and run!

August 20 - Undertrained? Enjoy the adventure!

Sure, it's great to line up for a race well-trained and optimistic, but it comes with the pressure of expectation. On the flip side, when you line up for a race that you are totally unprepared for, knowing you will perhaps walk more than run and it will be far from your potential, the stress is off. Low expectations allow for a different kind of adventure, one that can be as fun as a personal best effort and will still leave you with a story to tell. I'll be ready to hear your story, a story that might include how I tricked you into it running a race so unprepared!

Run it anyway.

August 21 - What is your 10K time?

What is your marathon time? You would think these are simple straightforward questions. Not! When asked such a question a runner will do some mental gymnastics to come up with an answer. Do you give your personal record time from 12 years ago? Do you give the time you hope to run next, the time you ran last, a ballpark time of about what you can run now? (Always erring on the fast side of course.) Worse yet, do you answer with an explanation of your entire running career, including your PR and your almost-times. (Yes, this describes me but I'm guessing I'm not alone on this.)The hard truth is that we are the runners we are today and the time we actually ran at a recent race, and more importantly, the race we are training for is what matters. Dang. So, get out there and train. The time that matters is before you. We can BS about the glory days when we grab a beer sometime.

No more living in the past, train for now.

August 22 - Adventure

There are risks and benefits that come with the adventure of our active lifestyles. We experience euphoric highs when we reach our goals due to our commitment, and the lowest of lows when our hard work fails us, feelings those living in a couch-potato haze will never know. We wouldn't want it any other way. The word adventure is from the Latin *adventura*, defined as when the outcome is uncertain, at the root of our passion and keeps the fire lit. We take risks when we head out to train, some we can control by being aware of the world around us and others we can't. Wearing reflective clothing, running against traffic, not wearing headphones, heading to a traffic-free shaded trail or park can reduce the risks, but are not always options to get the run done.

As you head out to train, please be careful out there and enjoy the adventure.

August 23 - Do you want to see my race medals?

I often bring up the importance of sharing the gift of running. That said, many of us may be just a bit too excited about our sport, especially while training for an event. Okay, what I mean is, you might just share my problem. We need to be sensitive to our nonrunning friends and family members who might not be excited to hear about our workouts, long runs, total weekly mileage, pace or race plans. Kind of like the golfer explaining their round hole by hole--painful. The best way to share our joy is to let them see that we are productive, fit, helpful and concerned. If they get the idea that our running contributes to that, the gift has been shared.

Speak with your feet.

August 24 - Savor the good days and store the memories for when the rain comes

Thanks to injury, sickness and all that life throws in our path, every healthy running day is a gift. We runners are like the Phoenix, after the crash we have the ability to look through the smoke and ash for a route that allows us to crawl back to standing. We then put one foot in front of the other until we are running once again. Our goals and training never end.

Get out there and put some hay in the barn.

August 25 - Don't let one bad run ruin the next

We all have runs that just plain go bad, be it dead legs, intestinal distress, fatigue or shortness of breath. For whatever reason, it happens. We might walk, cut it short or just bail out. The worst part about the bad run is the gun-shy feeling we have as we prepare to head out for the next run. Shake it off. Again, the answer is to get back on the horse, you know the magic is out there, but you won't experience it if you sit on your butt.

Once again, the answer is to get out the door. The magic will return and it will all be worth it, but only if you keep getting out that door. Sure, I've said this before but I'm talking about today!

So go!

August 26 - Am I a runner?

It' so easy to shortchange ourselves. Lacing them up and getting out the door consistently, even if it's one run per week, means you are definitely a runner and a dedicated runner at that. My guess is when we look at ourselves we tend to compare our running to people who run more than we do, not those who do less. Not looking at the whole picture, we sell our accomplishments short. If we look at all we do in a week in other areas of life, like family, business, and socially, then look at the commitment it takes to put in the weekly run, considering the physical and mental benefits these runs give us, we'll realize we are not only RUNNERS but smart and efficient ones!

This week's run will prove you are a runner.

August 27 - The sweet spot

As we increase our weekly mileage, we drag ourselves out the door day after day, often dreading the longer runs. When we finally get to the plateau, the new higher mileage level, it usually comes with a breakthrough run that has us heading happily out the door to run a distance that just a few months ago we would have dreaded. You can't beat the feeling of fitness. We work hard to get it, so when it comes, enjoy the spring in your step and don't forget to hang around the plateau awhile to enjoy it. Better yet, stay there the rest of your life!

Run until you reach nirvana.

August 28 - Let old habits die

Many of us runners are creatures of habit, running the same routes and sticking to the same equipment. For years, the water carrier I used on my long runs fit poorly, often dropped the bottles and I dreaded wearing it. Of course, it was expensive, had great reviews in all the run publications, and I saw others using the same pack all the time, so I bull-headedly soldiered on. I finally tried a new hand-held carrier that I no longer dread. Duh. Of course, I have yet to replace my running watch that never seems to stay on the function I want because the thing just won't die. Somebody smack me.

If it sucks, give it up. Do it today and enjoy the dang run like never before!

August 29 - Yes, you are a runner!

Again, I repeat the important stuff! I recently witnessed tears of joy from a first-time 5K trail run finisher. The steep hills and dirt footing made this a challenging adventure for many who were venturing off the roads for the first time. Each run is a stepping stone, a learning experience that moves us forward to the next adventure. Many of us saw the finish line of our first race as an affirmation, giving us the okay to say to the world, "I am a runner!" Great stuff. Yes, there were runners who ran longer races at the event and we were in awe of their commitment to the sport and the incredible mental and physical tenacity they had developed in their running lives. Finishers who had tears of joy in their eyes, the same tears of joy they experienced long ago when they crossed their first 5K finish line!

You are a runner, so run!

August 30 - Run, or jump out of a plane

Life can be tough, even when things seem to be going well. The stress from day-to-day life can lead to midlife crisis or at least put our mood into a funky dark hole. Yikes! What's the answer? I don't know for sure, but I'd bet something as simple as a bucket list can make a difference. What to put in there? My vote is for a half-marathon, marathon, triathlon, or ultra-marathon, which ever seems the most impossible to do. (What did you expect?) No matter how it goes, you will get a clean T-shirt to wear after the event! Go online to a race calendar and load up your bucket, or maybe you could buy a Harley, learn to pole dance or jump out of a plane!

Get out for a head-clearing run and start your list.

August 31 - I remind you, savor the pain. You worked hard to feel this bad!

Today's run was, to say the least, difficult. From the first step to the last, including the 3 times I had to walk a bit to catch my breath. It took all I had to keep moving forward. The planned 8 miles ended at 5.8. The pace was pathetic, but the effort to accomplish so little felt heroic, far more so than the finish of some marathons I have run. This painful struggle will no doubt be the highlight of my day. Only those who run can possibly understand why I'm wearing a smile after such misery.

Go earn some pain to savor.

September

September 1 - Don't waste your run

I found myself almost done with my run when I realized I had not once looked around at the wonder of the world around me and had not once listened to my footfalls or the sounds of nature. My mind remained abuzz, cluttered with all I should have left behind for the run to do its magic. I know that it takes a conscious effort to clear the head and live fully in the moment. I had ignored all the triggers that usually bring me to the place that I feel completely alive and living in full color. I came to a dead stop, took a deep breath, erased my thoughts and started to feel the right now, a feeling as good as it gets. All that said, at least the miles still counted!

Unlike me, don't waste a moment of today's run.

September 2 - Feeling a bit off?

I felt kind of off yesterday, so I blew off the run. Today, I started my day with the same blah feeling but decided to get out there and see if the run might change things up. It was a tough run with low energy, shortness of breath and it never got better. I was feeling bummed out, but finished as planned. Not thinking much more about it, I jumped back into my workday where I immediately got swallowed up with the regular growing to-do list. About an hour in I took a break to get out my lunch and it occurred to me that I felt great, no blah to be found! I then remembered, I got a run in! Dang, the run worked and just like with many drugs--it took a while to get into the system to do its work!

Today's run may be the cure.

September 3 - N=1, go run!

I repeat the important stuff. Don't let ego get in the way of your complete enjoyment of this running life! EVER! Even as an obsessed, life-long runner, when I read a Facebook post by someone who just ran a fast 15-mile training run or any run longer, faster or in conditions that I am currently not capable of running in, I can't help but start to compare myself and get my envy up. Worse yet, letting ego cause me to run with a friend or group at a pace or distance that I should not be running, risking injury. We can NEVER compare ourselves to others, we have different genetics and different life experiences that include past injuries, time restraints, responsibilities and countless variables that play a part in the unique person we are. We are a study of one (N=1). We need to remember how cool that is as we continue to learn who we are and where we fit into this world. We are each a unique puzzle piece. You, just the way you are, are needed to complete history!

This includes your run today!

September 4 - Trust reality: run!

I recently saw an article headline, *Why intensive jogging is just as unhealthy as being a couch potato.* This makes headlines? An online news article throws out a few sound bites from several studies and comes up with this headline, but with absolutely no data or facts. You've got to laugh at the term, "intensive jogging," whatever that means! Why does the media give attention to crap like this while diseases of a sedentary lifestyle place a huge burden on our healthcare resources, and contribute to early death? Do you think they are pandering to the majority? Duh. We don't run to escape death, we run to move, to enjoy the natural world and to have the energy necessary for a rich and wonderful life.

Only trust reality, get out and run.

September 5 - The dumbing down of running

Have you noticed the proliferation of articles and books with topics like, *Run less, run faster, Train only 3 days a week and finish a marathon*, or *Run your best race on only 10 miles per week*? It seems like there is a lot of dumbing down in all areas of our lives, including passions. I want you to know, it's okay to make a resolution to put in the highest running mileage year of your life or to put in the longest single run you have ever done! Perhaps put in the highest mileage ever while training for a specific race. Write a schedule and make it happen. You'll be faster, fitter and will get the kind of satisfaction not found with some wimpy attempt to just get by. The middle of the road will get you run over. Yikes! That said, it really is okay to get in the minimum, which is far better than most people who do nothing. I just wanted to let you know it's okay to strive to be the best.

Get out the door and hammer, or whatever you choose, just get out there.

September 6 - Running = Peace

With so much uncertainty, our running passion can be the constant that make sense out of a world that often does not seem to make any sense at all. In these fast-changing times, job security is a notion of the past, plus frequent technological advances that add stress to our lives as never before. And there is terrorism that is absolutely insane, a country so divided . . . you get the point. Running is always there for us, just out the door, ready to clear our heads. Running, an unplugged, back to the basics experience that resets us mentally and physically. When the world beats on us, it's great to know the run is there to soften the blows.

Keep your log, keep the faith.

September 7 - Binge running

It's become quite popular to binge-watch several episodes of the many TV series available today. Each of our runs is an episode in our running life. Today, my run ended on a high note, leaving me excited to see what tomorrows brings. Some days, the run goes so bad I'm afraid of what might come next. At these times I've even taken the next day off to shake off the feeling of impending doom. Then again, some runs are so amazing I re-run them in my head to experience and savor the glory once again. Here's a thought--if today's planned run of 5 miles goes well, how about passing the house and bingeing a second loop! Sure, you might cut into your time to watch *Fargo* or whatever, but you will be the star on today's run and will be an episode ahead!

Turn it off, head out the door and turn it on!

September 8 - The worst day of your life

When life slams you to rock-bottom, pulling off the daily run may be the most difficult move you can imagine. If you are feeling this way, it's time to block out the pain, the world and get out that door and let the run shoulder some of your burden. Perhaps if you instill this concept deep in your consciousness, it will propel you to make the first steps possible. Once out the door, your mind will be flooded with a million reasons you need to be anywhere but out running. If you avoid all thought for a second, everything the run has to offer will have a chance to fight its way in, perhaps offering you strength, clarity and hope, if even for a few minutes. Repeat over the days ahead. Our prayers are with you.

Think of this and make this tool a part of you during the run today.

September 9 - Lucky numbers

How far did you run today? Perhaps it's only me but certain numbers of miles just sound better. I like even-numbered runs but also runs divisible by 5. Okay, I also like 3 miles and 13 miles because they relate closely with 5K and the half-marathon. So, I would rather run 2, 3, 4, 5, or 6 miles but 7 and 9 don't do it for me, I'd rather end with 8 or 10. The number 11 is also a loser, along with 17 and 19. I actually arrange my route to be 12, 13, 14, 15, 16, 18 or 20. What does this have to do with motivating your butt out the door? Nothing, but perhaps giving this some thought will distract you from giving the run much thought, and by the time you realize it, you will be already out the door!

Go run whatever distance you darn well please today.

September 10 - Running is like a 3-chord rock song

As my British rocker friend Mike would say, most rock and roll tunes are just three moronic chords played over and over until something magical seems to happen. Much like running, where the nonrunner might say putting one foot in front of the other over and over seems rather moronic. As we continue to put in miles, running gets into our head and under our skin like a favorite tune we can't get out of our head. A tune we are happy to play again and again. Our moronically simple run motivates and fulfills us down to our core, like a great song only we runners can hear, mile after moronic mile.

Get out there; it's time to play it again!

September 11 - 9/11, a somber but hopeful day

I awoke on September 11, 2001 and turned on CNN to watch police; firefighters and rescue workers start an unending marathon of action, endless dangerous and exhausting shifts with no end in sight. The physical and mental pressures were hard to imagine, knowing that every minute that passed decreased the chances of saving lives. The unfolding situation struck many of us as we watched from afar. If it were in our backyards, would we be ready? Running gives us cardiovascular fitness and increased endurance and energy. Running increases our self-esteem and self-efficacy. Training and racing help us to learn long-term goal planning. Distance running teaches us patience. Running leaves us prepared for the best and the worst. Would you want to be the person helping, or the one who needed help?

Run, so you can be ready.

September 12 - Your run may save a life

Yesterday's theme continues. No matter how advanced we become as a society, there will be dangerous situations where your level of fitness could determine life or death. I was once in an accident situation where one person stayed to stabilize an injured person while one ran for help. No cell service was available, and time was critical. Rescue situations occur daily where strength and endurance save lives. And there will be situations where we become the first responders, maybe while out on a trail or remote road run where we come across a situation that our strength or speed could make all the difference.

Get out for a run, it may prepare you to save a life, perhaps your own.

September 13 - Run unafraid

When running alone I would find myself running through scenarios in my head of some idiot assaulting me and how I would respond. As runners we all have stories. I've been yelled at, had beer cans thrown at me, and I've had a confrontation with a guy on a mountain bike threatening to beat me up the next time I run on the trail in the same direction he rides. Recently, I took a self-defense class, and I can tell you it made a difference in my confidence. When you encounter a situation, you will naturally respond the way you are trained. A good class will give you common sense suggestions on how to react and will stick with you. It's a truly liberating feeling that will get you out the door with confidence.

Be prepared and run unafraid.

September 14 - You can do it anywhere

My daughter Anna, jumping in to spout some motivation.

As runners, we are blessed with the ability to practice our sport just about anywhere. There are a million excuses out there but one I'll not accept is "I can't get a run in HERE." Tomorrow I have an early flight, a busy day and I've already planned to get my miles in at the airport while I wait to board. Last weekend at work I couldn't be far from my desk, but you better believe I did laps around the parking lot! Deathly afraid of deer flies and afraid to run on the dirt road like I am? Try running laps around your yard or pace the driveway! You can get the miles in ANYWHERE so forget that excuse.

Get out there, wherever!

September 15 - A run back to 1918

I was reminded again what a wonderful adventure it is to find a new trail or historic neighborhood to run in. I met with The Martian Invasion of Races team last night in Dearborn, Michigan to look over some route changes for the Spring event. I arrived with time to get in an hour of running and found my way on the trails behind Fairlane Manor, the home of Henry Ford and Clara from 1915 until their deaths in 1947 and 1950. As I ran around stone gazebos, gardens and ponds on the sprawling estate, I imagined the Fords walking these same paths behind their new home, perhaps a hundred years ago to the day on a similarly cold, bright September afternoon. Never stop exploring on the run. Great finds will keep getting us out the door.

Do some exploring today.

September 16 - You are always in your prime

My wife and I have made a vow never to play the age card again--that is, bringing up age when talking about running, or anything! For example, "When I was in my twenties, I finished this race in the top 10," or, "Yeah, you were ahead of me, but wait until you're over 50," or any similar comment that uses age as an excuse. It has been refreshing to become ageless again and to enjoy running, competition and every day of life to the fullest extent possible. Ah, to be in my prime again! I'll be darned, I *am* in my prime! And to think, I get to stay here! Give it a try, you'll be hooked!

To heck with age groups, get out and run like the kid you are.

September 17 - Today's run might be the best ever, of course you know that!

I just returned from a blustery, beautiful run down a hilly, quiet, country dirt road. For me, it was perhaps as good as it gets. Every season, every run, and whatever the weather has in store offers an opportunity to experience this amazing world. Keep those priorities in order and get out the door. I'm sure you will be a better person for it so, no excuses!

Run on down, run on down, run on down a country road.

September 18 - Your Magic Kingdom

Nothing can compare to the daily run from home on a no stress, familiar course where we can get lost in our thoughts or seek the answers to life's difficult questions. We usually call this course "our course," of course! The fond memories of the route and the place it plays in the grand scheme of life will be etched in our minds forever. We won't remember each outing as they will blend together, but a mental journey to the old course will be like going home. As we run on vacation or as we travel the world, perhaps down the Champs-Elysees in Paris, through the National Mall in Washington D.C., around the castle in Disney's Magic Kingdom or down Ali'i Drive in Kona, none will quite compete with our home course as we reminisce. Thoughts of our course will give us a content feeling of satisfaction from a running life lived fully.

Run from your castle today, and smile at the plebs as you go by.

September 19 - Defense is the best offense

A young runner on a local cross-country team was hit by a car during a run in the early morning hours and is in critical condition. As we head into these shorter days, most of us will be running our miles in the dark. Be smart, wear a reflective vest, a headlamp and perhaps a red flashing strobe if you must run on the roads. I admit, running in the dark is pretty cool. I get a weird smug sense of satisfaction pounding out the miles as much of the world goes into a couch potato kind of hibernation. I wear a headlamp and carry a small LED flashlight to make my own daylight. Don't let darkness or weather stop your scheduled daily run. Plenty of other stuff will do that, but please run safe and light the night.

Be seen, be safe.

September 20 - It's never bad, always good, many times, great!

Every day gives us new reasons to be excited to be runners, like the perfect running temperature on a misty and mystical morning on the start of a delicious Fall day. The sight, sounds and smells of Autumn can be thick, as night slides away and daylight creeps in to join us. Perhaps tomorrow will be a repeat performance or perhaps it will be a gusty, rainy, cold, slap-in-the-face kind of run that comes to greet and challenge us. Bring it on, we are here for the wild ride and the satisfaction we get from getting out that door!

May today's run shake you up, in a good way!

September 21 - A bumpy ride

On the economic side, it looks like we are in for a continual wild ride and as I've said so often, we are fortunate to have running to get us though. With the mental and physical health we get from our runs we can better handle adversity. Running puts us in a better position to be a positive and helpful source for others as well as ourselves. We will all be looking for value in not only what we buy but also in what we do. Running will be a valuable use of our time; a great return on the time we invest each week. A short run can go a long way!

Make the down days up--run.

September 22 - No time for a run? Then make time for sickness

We live such busy lives that often we neglect our own body, forgetting that we are only as strong as our weakest link. We have no time for sickness. Heck, it's not even on our schedule! Like our cars, we expect our bodies to start up and take us where we want to go, until they won't. Schedule some daily healthy time for your body, or plan on unexpected time down or even early death, the same as our cars.

Our relationship with our body is like a marriage, an arranged marriage at that. We did not choose this body, but we are bound to it in sickness and in health, in good times and in bad, until death do we part. We need to make time for each other, listen to each other, work with each other and accept that nothing good comes easy. Make a run date with your body for tomorrow, then take it out for a healthy dinner!

Have a great run, and give that body a hug.

September 23 - Trust the miles

Last night I escaped the world for a bit as I was transported to the front of the pack of the 2010 Western States 100-Mile Endurance Run by watching the YouTube movie *Unbreakable.* Upbeat, motivational movies and books can change a negative thought pattern to one of hope and wonder. Seeing what the human spirit is capable of might give us the push needed to reach our potential. These vegan hippie athletes, the best long-distance runners in the world, who run 150 to 200-mile weeks up and down mountains, alone in the wilderness, have incredible insight, not unlike cloistered monks or gurus. A common thread was leaving structured training behind and trusting long hard miles with thousands of feet of climb on rocky rooted trails, letting the run teach us the way.

Trust today's miles.

September 24 - Pain, good or bad?

There are two very different schools of thought about pain. First is the "all pain is bad" gang, the sedentary folks who have avoided it their entire lives. Second is the "pain is only bad when I don't have control over it" group, the physically active crowd. We know that pain is not the opposite of joy because we actively pursue joyful activities, like running a race and accepting the pain as part of what it takes to be fulfilled. I believe the opposite of joy is lack of feeling. We savor the pain from a hard event. We worked hard to get that totally spent, beat-up feeling. The pain reminds us that we deserve some downtime, some well-earned rest and relaxation. Unnecessary downtime, like anything in life we don't earn, gives little satisfaction. I'm sure the sedentary folks get bored with lying around while we see the chance to chill as a precious gift, a bit of a reward that refreshes us so that soon we can leap up and go at it again!

Let's get out there and earn it.

September 25 - Run into the new day

Don't you love a Fall run that starts in the cold and dark, heads through a breathtaking sunrise, then, as the day quickly heats up, leaves you sweating like it's Summer and stripping down to the basics by the end? There is a bit of magic in a run that takes you from the cold to warm and night into the day. It's not easy to explain but it seems to give the satisfaction and feeling of a very long run--powerful, like a run that lasted 2 days!

Get out there.

September 26 - Hello darkness my old friend

As the days shorten many of us will be training in the dark. Always wear a reflective vest, carry a light, wear a headlamp, use a strobe light, run against traffic, or better yet, run where there is no traffic whenever possible. All the flashing lights in the world won't help you if a careless, distracted driver is veering out of their lane and coming your way. As I've said, I love the beauty and powerful feeling of running into the sunrise or sunset. I love running on a star-filled night with a crunch of snow underfoot. I love it all, but I also respect and accept the risks that can't be avoided as we head off into adventure.

I've come to visit you again.

September 27 - This run is for you

Written on the Temple of Apollo are the words, "Know thyself, and thou shalt know the universe and God." Running is wonderfully personal, and it allows us to spend quality time with ourselves and discover who we are. We alone know the effort we are putting into our runs and when the pace is easy or hard. Our personal records really are personal, they come from the bodies we were born with and the way we choose to train them. Yes, we can read and listen to coaches and others about how to train, but it comes down to what works for us, feels right, and fits into our complicated lives. When we follow our own path and accomplish our personal goals, it means more to us than any outside praise ever could.

Follow your path.

September 28 - How fast do you run a mile?

How fast we are is not relevant, it's our personal understanding of the work we have done to cover the distance we ran in the time it took us. Not just physical effort but also the mental effort, from our courage to start to the willpower to be consistent, doing something most people look at as punishment or even torture. Only the runner understands all that our sport gives back to us and how we can find joy in it. How fast do you run a mile? As fast as you want.

May we have the courage to continue running, forever.

September 29 - The ultimate investment

As I've said, the market might crash or soar but getting out the door for each day's miles is one of the rocks you can steady this life on, a recession-proof passion. In the lean years, we might not be able to afford to fly to Hawaii to run a marathon, but we can lace 'em up and head out the door for a head-clearing trip to nirvana with no cash needed. Running is a simple sport worth so much more than the sum of its parts, the ultimate investment. Go stash some miles away.

Run with the bulls.

September 30 - Spread the love or running

Last week on vacation I had a magic day where my family all ran together in a 5K from beginning to end. Running truly is a gift, and one that we can share. Invite (trick!) a non-running friend to enter a 5K with you. Enter a race that has walkers and promise you will stay with them from beginning to end, walking, running, whatever. Explain that the intimidation of entering an event may seem like a huge obstacle, but they will soon realize it DOES NOT EXIST! Get them out there and they will see people of every shape and age walking, running, plodding and having fun! A simple 5K can be a catalyst that changes lives.

Change the world.

October

October 1 - Yes, you can

In 1980, my new bride and I were sitting on our couch watching an IRONMAN® event on *Wild World of Sports*. I could only imagine what these athletes were thinking as they lined up in the water waiting for the starting cannon to fire, knowing what a long and painful day was before them. When the show ended, my wife turned to me and said, "I could do that, we should do that." I said nothing, my head needed time to process the comment. She was serious. My wife swam in college and had become a solid runner. We biked, but not too seriously, just a long charity ride or two. I said, "Okay." Immediately, I knew this was a big deal but I had no idea how much that response would change our lives forever, and no longer did I have to wonder what it was like to hear that starting cannon in Kona.

Just say okay.

October 2 - Some days you need to be a wimp

Especially for those of you in long-race training mode, when you get to that last long run on the schedule, remember, your body is out on that crumbling edge, just about ready to break. Your chances of getting injured are at an all-time high. You need to not volunteer when it comes to moving a heavy object, pushing out a stuck car, or whatever. No weekend warrior activities like doing a big day of lawn work. Yes, it sucks, but you worked hard to get here, and it's time to be a wimp. That said, I just ran my last long run. I'm sick as a dog, and I pulled a quad muscle putting screens up in my attic--some coach, eh?

Next, we taper!

October 3 - Time to reap

Time to reap the benefits of the year's training miles and crank in a Fall race, unless you are like me, coming off a Summer drought and sidelined by injury. Luckily, I started a late crop of miles that seem to be coming in nicely as I become pain-free. No personal records this Fall but I'll do what I can and I'm hungry for next year. I'm getting in miles and that's good for now. For the rest of you with a barn full of hay, enjoy the fruits of your harvest and run a great one!

Put the hammer down and burn that hay!

October 4 - It's okay to enjoy the taper

With the long races coming up, many of you will face the taper. For those of you newer to distance racing, we taper our training miles down the days (weeks) just before an event. The taper gives us time to lick the high mileage training wounds and rest up, storing the glycogen needed to get us to the finish line. During the taper we find ourselves with extra time on our hands, time to worry about our training, our race, and what we eat, darn. May I share some taper tips, starting with-- enjoy it! You worked hard to get here; use the extra time to read a motivational book, watch a motivational movie, get a massage and take a nap. I guess you could be responsible and catch up on work you got behind on during training, dang. As you drop your mileage, up the tempo. This is called sharpening. These final short fast runs will make long race pace feel slow and easy.

Bring on the taper!

October 5 - Eat, eat, eat, run, run, run

On the way into work I passed a McDonald's billboard with the slogan: "When you need just a little more," referring to adding more burgers from the dollar menu to an already oversized meal. I also passed a Taco Bell that advertised: "4th meal, late night food." On the way home I passed a billboard for smart liposuction, ironically, across from the McDonald's billboard. I'm guessing the price of adding a few dollar menu items would pale in comparison to the price of "Smart Lipo!" So as long as you don't skip your run, you can eat the burger and skip the lipo!

When you need a little more, tack on some miles!

October 6 - Gear up for all conditions now, so no conditions offer an excuse!

The changing of the seasons adds some excitement to our simple sport. On the warm days, dressing to run is mindless, just wear as little as possible, but when the temperature drops, some thought is necessary to enjoy the run. I move to a long sleeve wicking base layer as we go into the 50s, and as it dips to the mid-40s to 30s, on come the gloves, hat, tights and perhaps a vest or jacket depending on the wind. For the snow, I wear Yak Tracks for traction and start to layer up. Now is the time to prepare, so the transition to Winter will not keep you from getting in your run, but will add to your running adventure! Don't forget the headlamp and reflective gear. All in all, pretty simple stuff, but you have to get it together. Dark and cold, here we come!

Be prepared.

October 7 - A body in motion stays in motion

As I headed out for the run this morning, I had nothing but negative thoughts--it's dark, it's cold, I have so much other stuff to get done. In reality, the sun would soon be up. It was not a wicked Winter day, and if I skipped the run now, I would not get to work that much sooner, and I'd be cutting out at lunch or earlier to run anyway. So, knowing this, and that once out the door I would eventually get into the groove, love the run and be happy and satisfied that I did run, it still took what seemed to be a serious effort to get out the door. The moral of the story--it's never easy but always worth it, and all that wasted negativity I started the day with was just that, a waste. Somebody smack me. I'll do the same for you if it helps!

Just get out and run, now!

October 8 - Fall, a two-edged sword

To write a get-out-the-door motivational message during these glorious Fall days may seem a wasted effort to some, but good days are fleeting and we will soon have to get in our runs during the cold, dark and wet mornings or evenings. As daytime continues to shrink, ugly days outnumber Indian Summer ones. It won't be easy, but always worth it. Do I sound like a broken record? A high lumen LED headlamp, along with an even brighter hand-held light can tear a hole through the dark and by overdressing a bit, the punch of the cold can be reduced to a light slap that we can defend against, giving us the edge to win round one of this six-month fight. I'm in your corner and cheering like mad!

We shall win the cold war.

October 9 - Put hay in the barn or fix the tractor

I hope you're having a Fall, full color, fully awake and alive kind of week in running! The sights, smells and sounds of October along with crisp mornings, sun-filled days and clear nights that sparkle, are as good as it gets. The roads and trails are calling, let's get out and grab the good ones. That said, for those of us who took our body to the crumbling edge in training this Summer and didn't pull it off, (injured, sick and in a funk), we can all relate to your pain. It's a risk and rewards running lifestyle we choose, offering the highest highs and the lowest lows, but we wouldn't want it any other way. Knowing that the other option is less personal growth and a guaranteed gray and boring road through this existence tells us we made the right choice, even when have to miss these few glorious days.

It is what it is, run if you can.

October 10 - Bully-free zone

My daughter, who calls herself a "not that obsessed runner," claims that growing up in a family of obsessed runners can be a little intimidating, so she offers this advice. "Lately on my runs, I've been bullying myself. I go faster than I want to, and push when something feels wrong, and it has been making it harder to get out the door each day! Getting out the door is hard enough, so I am putting in the work this week to STOP bullying myself. I'm not bullying myself into somebody else's pace when I don't feel it, I'm not pushing my heart rate up where it doesn't need to be. If something doesn't feel right, or if I can't breathe, I'm taking a walk break! Heck, at least I got out there."

Getting out the door is hard enough, so make your daily run a BULLY-FREE ZONE!

October 11 - Reinvent your run

There are events called "The Backyard Ultra," where the competitors run a 4.167 mile loop, on the hour, every hour, until there is only one runner left. If you are not lined up at the starting line on the hour, you are out. The 4.167 mile distance makes for a total of 100 miles in 24 hours. The current record is 67 hours and around 280 miles. Yikes! I have found that using a variation of this makes for an inspiring way to get in a very long run. Pick any distance loop and any time limit. Say, 1 mile in 10 minutes. Finish in 9 minutes, rest, stretch, get a drink or whatever, then head out at 10 minutes, again at 20 minutes, until you can't make it to the start line. Even more fun is to do this with a group of friends. Another variation is to reduce the time for each loop by one minute. For example, start with a 13-minute limit for loop one, 12 minutes for loop 2, etc. As the limit gets shorter, your rest period eventually evaporates. Dream up your own system and shake up your next long run!

May today's run blow your mind!

October 12 - We are all naturally beautiful, dig it

We live in a world obsessed with weight, body image, and diets. According to EatingDisorderHope.com, eating disorders are on the rise around the world. And the money spent on weight-loss products, diets and fat reduction surgery has grown. According to Worldometers.info, Marketdata-Enterprises.com esti- mates the U.S. weight loss market to be $60 billion and growing. As runners and walkers, we are far from immune to this obsession and the many negative and even dangerous and addictive aspects of it. It's not like we don't know this stuff, but I find it helpful to be reminded so we can take stock and be honest with ourselves. Weight comes down to calories consumed, calories burned and the genetically pre-disposed bodies we have. Stay active and get out the door. Enjoy the physical and psychological benefits of the run on a regular basis and look for the joy it adds to your life. With our different genetic makeup and our own life story, we get in trouble when we compare. Forget body image and learn to love the body you have and appreciate the differences between us all. We are fast, slow, tall, short, big-breasted, flat-chested, bald, hairy, thin, heavy, etc. Our differences are interesting and endless, like the differences in wine and food! Enjoy!

Fast or slow, love yourself and love your run!

October 13 - A final focus, read the night before your Fall long race

The event is at hand, the outcome is certain, there are no doubts. Trained or untrained, you will prevail. Think of the training you have done. The bad days, the good days. Every mile you covered in training will be there tomorrow to help you. Every mile you missed in training means nothing. You are here, you are committed, you will finish! Tonight, before you head to bed, take some time alone to go over your game plan. Think of tomorrow's weather, prepare for everything. Lay out your gear, and then put it on. Pin on your number, check everything. Knowing everything is there and everything is ready will allow you to get some sleep. No questions are unanswered. Forget the event, forget about everything--it's done, think sleep. You will awake ready. Remember the rituals you have developed, double-check everything. Clear your thoughts and savor the excitement of the start, store it in memory. The early miles are a time to socialize, a time to enjoy. Mile by mile, check to see that your pace is under control. Too fast? Slow down; take fluids. As the miles get long, it's time to concentrate. Focus on form, fluids, and pace. Enjoy the power you have to go on regardless of how your body feels. Let the confidence build. In the late miles, things will get tough. You know that; you will be ready. You will also be tough. Concentrate; avoid negative thoughts and negative people. Bear down and keep moving. The finish is in sight. Finish strong and proud.

Good night, sleep well.

October 14 - Let's play hooky

Running takes self-discipline and gives us a working understanding of long-term goal planning and delayed gratification. It's no wonder we are a hardworking, responsible gang--good stuff. That said, some of us need to recognize that being so productive can take a toll on us and that we really do deserve to blow a day off and play hooky. I suggest watching the weather and when a perfect Fall day is predicted, don't set the alarm, turn off your phone, get up when you wake up and head out to someplace fun for a run and see where the day takes you from there. Sure, our busy schedules and to-do lists don't allow for this, which is exactly why we need to do it!

Be a running bum for a day.

October 15 - No cramming for the exam

With cooler morning temps, it's time to put on the long sleeves, and it's a reminder that the Fall long race season is upon us and we may be behind in our training. I'm sure we're not alone on this; life sometimes gets in the way of our run schedule. Yes, we are getting out the door and putting in the daily runs, but perhaps not the long runs or mileage we hoped for, dang. Running is not a sport that we can "cram for the exam." We can only line up with the training we have put in or not. Don't bail on your event! Lining up under-trained guarantees an adventure! We may run some and walk more than some, but if we keep up constant forward progress we will get it done! Yes, our times will be pathetic, but nobody really cares. We will party when we finish (hopefully by last call)! If you are trained, go hammer!

Run and get it done.

October 16 - Look for clues

I read a Facebook comment, "Sure glad I got my miles in today before I came down with this awful cold." As runners, this is the mentality that leads to days off due to sickness or pain. A smart comment would be, "I sure wish I had skipped today's run, I might have been able to duck getting sick." Our sport requires us to read our bodies closely, looking for clues that tell us when to back off, drop out of a race or train and race hard. We follow schedules, have weekly mileage goals and some of us even share this on social media, all of which brings pressure to perhaps sneak in just one more mile--often when we know we are pushing the limit—which might cost us a month of mileage, dang.

Let's run as smart as we can.

October 17 - Hire a runner

Runners have energy, endurance, are self-directed and understand long-term goal planning. We take what we learn in training and use these skills in our work and family life. Our daily run and our work bring new challenges every day, we take hills head-on and push to the top of each one until we are totally spent, then we dig to discover more within us and go the extra mile. If you want something done, hire a runner! There is also a good chance a runner will take fewer sick days. That said, you might have to install a shower for maximum efficiency. Live and work like you run.

Add today's run to your resume!

October 18 - Permission to blow off your run today, if it makes sense

We are only as strong as our weakest link. This is a hard concept for passionate runners, when running seems so complete on its own. The reality is that we use the same muscles through the same range of motion, causing imbalance and reduced flexibility. One false step out of our normal range of motion or a strength requirement beyond what our running calls for and we are toast. So, I give you permission to blow off the day's run, ONLY if you replace it with a decent session of core work like yoga, strength training, planks, lunges or similar nonaerobic torture. Dang.

Run complete.

October 19 - Everybody dies, not everybody lives

I've heard that running, like red wine, may not make us live longer. Actually, as I think about it, if I didn't run it might feel like life would drag on forever, and a life without red wine? You get the point. I do get a kick out of sound bite news stories like the one I heard this week stating that sad people live just as long as happy people, perhaps a relief to somebody. But it seems even sadder to me. Okay, today I'm just rambling, time to stop reading.

Smile and get out there.

October 20 - Don't run like a freshman

Most world records in long events are set with negative splits, that is, running the last half of the race faster than the first. A simple concept is to feel as good as you can as long as you can, then put the hammer down. Unfortunately, this is much harder to practice than to preach. We come into the race tapered, refreshed and ready. The early miles feel effortless, even though as we get the split times we know they are faster than what we had planned. So, we start thinking of the time as money in the bank and slow up after a bit and get into a groove, but the damage has been done. Soon there is a run on the time bank. Holding our pace through the late miles is always hard, and going out fast has made it impossible. Nobody wants to hear about any of your great split times, only your finish time. As for this motivating you for today's run, negative splits not only have a place in your race, but consider going out for today's run a bit slower than planned and finish a bit faster than planned. Then smile at your finish time and average pace!

Run smart.

October 21 - Obsessed running loser

I usually get out for a run before attempting to write an inspirational piece, but due to an ugly, medial collateral ligament, I'm composing this at a time when I'm not able to put in miles. I admit it's hard not to feel like a loser and a charlatan while writing as the obsessed runner, but not to worry, I'll recover, and I do have a diversified portfolio to keep up the endorphins and reduce my losses. I can ride a bike, put in laps in the pool and get my yoga buzz on. Perhaps this week's message will be a good reminder for all of us to do our core work. Let this also be a sympathetic message for those of you on the sidelines: you are not alone! For you healthy people, do not use this message as any kind of lame excuse for not getting your butt out the door, putting in the hard work and lining up to test yourself at the weekend races!

Recover smart and if you can run, RUN, or I'll be pissed off!

October 22 - The trail is my coach

Thirty-four years ago my friend Jeff introduced me to a trail near my home, a 13-mile hilly monster that goes past a dozen lakes in a Pure Michigan wonderland, a trail that to this day continues to beat me up and keep me honest. The trail is my home turf, my loop. When I run the trail affectionately known as "Poto," it brings on a flood of memories. At times I'll remember exactly what I was thinking at the exact same points on the trail, perhaps on a similar day 10 years earlier. These thoughts will often intertwine with whatever my current day's thoughts or worries are and help to ground me and give me answers. The trail is my coach, it reminds me every time I run it that if I let my fitness level slip, the trail will not be within my capabilities, yikes!

May you find a route that keeps you in the game.

October 23 - Celebrating 2 million years of obsessed running!

Humans have been running around the planet for around 2 million years, living on the front lines, chasing down dinner and celebrating the survival of another day. Evolution tweaked us into amazing running machines. My guess is that until the arrival of modern civilization, women and men both put in 70 to 100-mile weeks of running at a level that today we would call world-class. That said, for our running future as a species, it's time to use it or lose it. Let's get out and hammer! It's time to protect what we've been blessed with and pass it on.

Run and evolve to perfection.

October 24 - The elusive rave run

Some runs just suck, and some runs are okay, but I just had my first fast, fun and amazing-feeling run in a while and can honestly say it was worth the wait. Rave runs like these, sometimes few and far between, keep getting us out the door. Kind of like pulling the slot machine handle over and over, or casting a line just one more time, hoping for the magic to strike.

May you hit the jackpot on today's run.

October 25 - Run aware, run with care

An old friend and amazing athlete was killed when she was struck by a truck while out on a training ride. Tragedy is a harsh reminder of how fragile and precious life is, a brutal reality check of the risks we face every day as part of our active lifestyle. All the cool things in life seem to come with a bit of risk and danger, but missing out on them can bring on stress and depression. The answer is to respect the risks, mitigate them to the best of our abilities and head out the door to live life fully. When you head to the trails, parks and woods, find a running friend, ditch the headphones, alter your routes, always run against traffic and respect the weather. Stay alert at all times and don't flip off the jerks even though they deserve it. Dang.

Run aware, run with care.

October 26 - Does a fart ever leave a room?

Many of us live and work in a world that separates us from the earth and the natural environment. We go from a temperature-controlled home to a temperature-controlled building and end up spending most of our lives inside. We re-breathe stale, used air, walk on carpet and cement and rarely come in direct contact with the earth itself. This type of existence, without the addition of an outdoor passion, detaches us from the simple wonders of the world. Perhaps the most important aspect of the run is that it gets us outside. We feel the sun, wind and elements against our skin, we breathe in the sights, smells and sounds of the natural world and we get to look at all of creation, not just what was built by man. Without the run, how much time would we spend outside every day? As Winter moves in, getting outside for the run becomes even more essential, while almost everything else in our world moves indoors. The reality is you can always dress and be comfortable in cold conditions, it's only on hot days that our options get limited. Now is time to get your Winter run gear in order so you don't miss a minute of all that is amazing out there!

Get outside!

October 27 - Tears and Strength

Memorable days that stick with us forever are precious and all too few. As I worked the finish line at a recent marathon, I saw radiant smiles, tears of joy, tears of pain and expressions of emotions way over the top, like runners falling to their knees in prayer, kissing the ground and the raising of fists like in the *Rocky* movie. For sure, I was witnessing life-long memories being stored, memories that will be revisited throughout life to once again bring smiles, tears and strength.

Gonna fly now!

October 28 - Savor the pain

After a Fall marathon, we feel beat-up and complete. It was anticipation, hard work, worry and focus followed by the sweet spot, the accomplishment and peace that comes with it. For now, savor the pain. We worked hard to feel this bad. As I say all the time, we get to experience the true highs and lows of life, not that numb middle-of-the-road, couch-potato, comatose haze of constant blah. We know the full range of what life has to offer. Dig it! We are alive and know it; we'll stop when they throw the dirt on. The sedentary world will never understand.

Ease back slowly.

October 29 - Time is precious

Personal time is precious in this busy world and there is no better way to spend it than on the daily run. The satisfaction we get from our effort, pace, distance covered and dedication to our sport assures us that we did not squander the gift. We return to our hectic lives mentally charged and ready to share ourselves (better selves) with the world again. Running is the gift that keeps on giving, and It gets better. On race day, our personal pursuits come together as we share our pain, pleasure, glory and even defeat, taking the running experience to the astral plane, elevating the joy of a life fully lived to a place unexplainable to the nonrunning world.

Use your time wisely, now.

October 30 - Spooky weather

This morning, my wife and I left the warmth of our house and ran into a pounding 30-something degree rain. The 40 mph gusts cracking at the trees overhead, the muddy trails under foot and the spooky daytime darkness in the woods made for the perfect Halloween run, a run that left us deserving of candy! We questioned heading out and waffled a while due to the wicked day, but we reluctantly decided it would be our only chance to run. We overdressed and headed out, running short but got 'er done. The moral of the story: Yes, not until we were out the door did we get into the spirit. Once outside, we laughed at ourselves and splashed along like happy campers, finishing totally fulfilled.

Trick yourself out the door for the treat.

October 31 – From Anna

GET OUT THE DOOR! I've rolled my eyes at my dad with this mantra more times than I can count. But I'm going to let you in on a little secret. I've been in a bit of a rut with my running. I am 16 weeks into a training plan and I'm beat! Last week I sucked it up and finally boarded the get-out-the-door train. I hate to say he told me so, but my miles are up, my spirits are up, and I think I'm on my way out of this rut! Was there a lot of walking involved? Sure! Did I randomly PR a 10K on a Wednesday? YUP! It doesn't matter what you achieve out there, but I urge you to put your shoes and a smile on, don't look too hard at your watch or your schedule and have some FUN! A note from the Obsessed Runner's daughter Anna, who is campaigning to make running FUN again, join me!

Get out the door!

November

November 1 - Why run in this crap?

As I look out at this gray, rainy, windy day I realize I'll need to strengthen my resolve to enjoy running through the cold months, especially November, when it is often frigid, wet and blah. How's that for an inspirational start? Heading out the door on a day that looks just awful is never easy, but once the heart rate steadies and we get in the mantra of our footfalls, the simple beauty of the natural world often shines through. From the pattern of rain on the puddles to the wild swirl of wind in the trees, we pound on. The reality is that running is an extreme sport, a tough and challenging sport that never lets up, a sport not for the faint of heart. And for these same reasons, running is our lifeblood, it gives us self-confidence and we find strength in ourselves we might have missed with a less daunting choice to direct our passion. We become the strong, determined, dedicated people our sport requires us to be, making us the ones who can get things done. Through running, we learn to see past the seemingly impossible problems of the world, making us the ones who might find the solutions that will change the world for the better.

Bring it on!

November 2 - The ugly running days

November weather is usually consistent--consistently MISERABLE! Yes, it's the start of what I call the off season, but a goal of getting out the door at least every other day is in order. No mileage goal needed, once you get out the door that part works out fine, just get out the door. Remember, all runs are good runs once they are over! Yes, I do repeat the important stuff!

Pull 'em on, lace 'em up, and you know what.

November 3 - Thoughts on sharing our run socially

I admit, I spend a bit of time each day on Facebook runner lists I've joined. I enjoy rave run posts that get me excited to get out and run new, wild places. I search out posts that give first-hand accounts of event experiences, yes, for the review value but more for when the writer captures the essence of each step of their personal journey. This can be powerful. That said, when someone new to running asks a question on these forums, the answers seem to come mostly from other new runners who are quick to share what is often horrible advice, which makes me cringe. Yikes! Got a question, look to coaches and long-time healthy, happy runners. Send a personal message to someone with a great track record and love for the sport. They will feel appreciated, give you good advice and be proud to be part of your success.

Close the dang computer and run.

November 4 - Hope springs eternal

The weather sucks, but we just have to ignore it and get out the door, like we always do! Work, money, power and war are similar to bad weather but once again, when we head out for a run, we find true peace in the moment. The gray sky seems not so gray and the nonsense of the world takes a back seat. What does this prove? Perhaps the run is the important part of our life and the rest is the nonsense we should strive to escape. The world may never be at peace and the sun may not come out for months, but we can be out running and living a fulfilling, fun life in the moment. We have won.

The run can be the sun, get out and enjoy it, with or without sunblock!

November 5 - Runners, we are as tough as they come

We get out the door on our own without fanfare or encouragement, day after day in any and all conditions, from scorching days to sub-zero blasts. There are no easy miles, they are all hard work. Our runs do not include rest breaks and our hearts pound on from beginning to end. Our sport is their sport's punishment, what they consider brutal is all we do. We speak with our feet. Our numbers don't lie; no judge is needed. There are no points for style and no cheering crowds. We are the toughest athletes in the world.

Go prove it.

November 6 - The best day to run is today!

Unlike so many other sports, our running season never comes to an end. We don't have to pack away our gear at the end of the year because there are 365 days and every day is ours! The seasons change and today we might bring cold running gear to the top of the pile, but it's a wonderfully simple sport, so it all fits on a shelf or two. The best time of year to run and the best day to run is always TODAY! All we have to decide is how far and what to wear. That said, Fall is pretty dang special, ha.

Run like there will be no tomorrow.

November 7 - Run, it's a blessing

This running and fitness lifestyle is a blessing. I cannot imagine life without a passion, better yet, a positive passion. I was driving behind a truck with lots of stickers about field training dogs, dog events, even a dog vanity plate. Much of it made no sense to me, much like a 26.2 sticker might not make sense to them, but you could feel the passion. The meaning of life? Perhaps not, but certainly an important part to a fulfilled and complete life is to make getting out the door a priority you don't want to mess with! Get out and run; it is essential for your happiness and wellbeing. How's that for justification!

Run, be fulfilled and if you want to, put an oval sticker on your car.

November 8 - Escape to reality

I believe many of us have been looking at running as an escape from reality, when in reality, running is an escape *to* reality! We start the preparation of escape by shedding our business attire and trappings of a complicated life. We then put on our feather light, technical play clothes and footwear, a subtle change that adds to the feeling of escape and prepares us mentally to take those first steps. We may run for 20 minutes or perhaps an hour, enjoying the endorphin flow and sweet rhythm of our body. This is followed by personal gratification, but it does not end there. Post run, the warm feeling in the chest and legs along with feelings of rejuvenation and satisfaction (the running buzz) takes hold and lingers for hours. Beyond this, the toning of the body and the new level of fitness we have given ourselves is like a suit of armor, making it possible to take on whatever the world throws our way. Dig it!

Escape to reality, now!

November 9 - I can because I run

A wise old runner said, "I don't run because I can, I can because I run." Our fitness level gives us access to so much life has to offer. We can fly up a flight of stairs or park in the far corner of the lot at Costco and skip the tangle of cars vying for a front row spot. We can visit New York City and take in all the sights on foot, walking from Battery Park to Central Park. Yes, running can add years to our lives and life to our years. According to the article, "Running Can Double Your Chances of Making it to 85" (*Runner's World*, March 2019, by Jordan Smith) people with high levels of fitness at 75 were twice as likely to live another 10 years than those sedentary lifestyles. That said, my own study revealed that runners experience more joy and happiness than dead people!

Get out and live.

November 10 - No excuses, not even great ones

Most of us are mired in our lifestyles with responsibilities of family, jobs, bills, piles of unfinished work and projects that could stop us in our tracks as we jump out of bed for the daily run. It is as if the enemy is trying to thwart our attack on each new day. We plan to wake up and run, a plan the world wants to sidetrack within minutes. The truth is, getting out the door is never easy and at times, just getting started requires a super-human effort. You have blown through that barrier plenty of times, the trick is to keep up the momentum, know thy enemies and defeat them every day!

Never give in; never give up.

November 11 - Freedom does not come free

If our day-to-day lives seem complex and stressful, I can only imagine the what difficulties and stress our U.S. military troops face, around the clock for their entire tours of duty in Iran, Afghanistan and every other dangerous place they are sent. Keep them in your thoughts and prayers on Veterans Day and every other day they are out there on the line for us. I get emails from the troops from time to time, letting me know that their daily runs, which are sometimes few and far between, let them escape the seriousness of their lives, giving them a calm moment to move, sweat and clear the head.

Today, dedicate your run to those who gave all so we can run free.

November 12 - Smug self-satisfaction

When spoiled by a mild start to November that has not helped us adapt to cold days to come, this will make it a bit harder to get out the door. I find it helps to overdress to reduce the cold slap in the face that might have kept us inside. Wearing a light pack allows us to shed layers and also to put them back on if needed, which can relieve our internal thermostat issues and make the run a lot less intimidating. Yes, the Winter laundry pile can get ugly, dang. All that said, a successful, brutal Winter run can build our self-esteem like no other. We will need to control our desire to give others the smug look of self-satisfaction as we plow on. The frost build-up on our face and hat should suffice!

The worse the better, bring it on.

November 13 - Watch some TV

Did you know that watching TV can be good for your running? It only happens a few times each year when the Olympics, world championships or a major marathon is on. After watching the best in the world and seeing the passion and commitment first-hand, you can't wait to get your butt out the door and try to be better than you are. We can't all be Olympians, but we can all be role models and heroes. How many times have you heard a neighbor say, "Aren't you the one I see out running every morning?" Yes, you are setting the example that in this busy world you fit in your run, perhaps making them pause to think, "Maybe I can do this too." Heck, invite them!

Watch TV, run and set the example.

November 14 - We made front page news!

It's nice to see running show up in the sports section, where spectator sports seem to be all that matters to the world. First, a sub two-hour pace marathon run by Olympic gold medalist and world record holder Kipchoge--yes, just a publicity stunt by a man who has nothing to prove, not a true record due to drafting, pacing and all they did to make it happen, but it made for some great press! A day later, Brigid Kosgei shattered the women's world record in the marathon with a 2:14, a record that stood for 16 years. Unlike all the sports that most of the world follows from an armchair and have never competed in, we have a true connection with world class runners. We train and compete, we understand commitment and how it feels to get out the door while the world sleeps, and we know what it's like to push our bodies to their limit. When our sport makes the news, we, in a sense, also make the news. Heck, without us, they would not have headlines like, *Kipchoge prevailed, coming in 1st ahead of 42,000 runners.* Hey, we are those runners!

November 15 - Get out and bask in the glory!

I've got a long history of being notoriously terrible at training. I write up crazy programs that I am unable to maintain and generally end up giving up and doing all of my work on race day. (OUCH!) I got a crazy idea this Fall--I wrote myself a totally realistic, do-able training schedule that leaves enough time for me to build up my mileage slowly. You know what? I have only missed ONE run in 8 weeks. I always joked that training just wasn't my thing, but the truth is I was overdoing it, which led to training failure after training failure when I couldn't keep up with my plan. Making a schedule that doesn't jump mileage over 10 percent week to week, and acknowledging how many available days in a week I actually have has made all the difference.

Get real with your training!

November 16 - We are not bullet proof, dang

Running may not add years to our life but it does add life to our years. The physical and mental benefits are many and I feel finding our way into this running life is a gift. All that said, a recent heart attack death of a 54 year old woman after a workout was a harsh reminder that we need to take the time to do the health screening that looks for any hidden medical issues that might put our active lives at risk. I've always said, stress tests are a pretty cool workout! A chance to take ourselves to the edge of collapse and to gain some confidence in our ticker's well-being. If you haven't, get 'er checked!

Run with medical confidence!

November 17 - Dare to be great, again!

You will always remember your first long race or triathlon, but if it was a while ago, just how much? Yes, it may have been life-changing and left you with skills you use daily, like long-term goal planning, an understanding of delayed gratification, excellent time management and perhaps healthy changes in your diet. Crossing the finish line might still be a vivid memory, but how about the feeling you got when you signed up and committed? Or the way the upcoming event was constantly on your mind and, in many ways, defining who you were? This is a reminder, a reality check, YOU CAN have that living-life-in-full-color feeling again! You can blow away the cobwebs from the often mind-numbing day-to-day lives we fall into. You can commit again and shake up your world! Perhaps an ultramarathon or trail marathon to light your fire? Just do it!

Kaboom!

November 18 - Keep it fun and get it done

Yesterday I had a fun point-to-point run, something I don't do often enough. There is a strange motivational quality to running someplace as opposed to ending up where you started. I guess that makes sense at some level, duh. Due to the nature of a point-to-point run, once you start, you are all in. If you're headed home, headed to work or whatever, you will need to finish this run no matter what. When there are high winds, running point-to-point can make for a pleasant run on an ugly day. That said, yesterday was a beauty and my run was a bit uphill and into a light headwind, still, a rewarding run all around, adding to my sense of accomplishment and adventure. I need to remember to ask more often, "Hey, which way are you headed? Do you mind dropping me off along the way?"

Turn your loop into a straight line today.

November 19 - The run accepts all

The daily run is not liberal or conservative, has no religious affiliation and has no enemies. The daily run can help lower blood pressure, contribute to cardiovascular health and has many other physical and mental health benefits. Rich or poor, in good times or in bad, the daily run is accessible to us all. Running events are celebrations of the human spirit, bringing together millions of people who support each other and share common goals and aspirations.

The daily run is yours and is just outside that door.

November 20 – That darn ego!

During the COVID-19 lockdown months I ran far more miles than normal, injury and pain-free. I kept waiting for the inevitable issues that arise when we up our miles substantially. Nada. Giving it some thought, I ran most of the miles alone or with my wife who runs a similar pace to mine and there were no races on the schedule. Unlike meeting up to run with a group or lining up to put the hammer down, all the miles were based on how I felt like running, no pushing through it, no keeping up, never running a pace based on the pace of others. My conclusion, when it's said to listen to the body, perhaps the louder voices of ego in our heads drown out that little voice that it trying to warn us of trouble.

Run, listen, and run forever.

November 21 - Only and Ego have no place in our running life

I recently used the word "only" to describe my day's run to a sedentary friend who had asked how far I had run. As I said it, it struck me that they may find this description arrogant and perhaps demeaning to their lifestyle. Dang. Another bad habit I have is to use the words, "you should." To change the world through running, something I believe in, we need to share our passion wisely.

As I have said, best to speak with our feet.

November 22 - It's time for the off season

Running is that sweet spot of our day, it's what we do to escape work, worries and stress. So, when I say stress-free running, it's a bit of an oxymoron but it's not that black and white. Following a running schedule and preparing for an event takes dedication and commitment and it comes with a certain kind of stress. I call it a self-imposed good stress that we control, but it's still real. That said, from now until the end of January, lighten up and enjoy! The serious events are over but the fun family running events can fit in well with the holiday schedule. If you haven't already, I suggest starting some holiday running traditions to get the family out together and share some fun miles. It starts with the turkey trots and holiday hustles and ends with St. Pat's runs. Then back to work, back to the controlled stress that takes us to greatness!

Run, relax, start a tradition.

November 23 - Go slog one out

Actually, with every run, no matter how short, far, fast or slow, our efforts are rewarded with a peaceful inner feeling, increased fitness and afterglow of personal satisfaction. Never do we feel like we wasted our time, even with a 12-minute slog in the slop! I do admit that the laundry we pile up this time of year, especially for a short run, sucks. The feelings we experience after our daily runs are cool. The feelings we get after a race we plan for, train for, and meet our goals are the pearls of life that get etched in our memories, stand the test of time and become a part of who we are. That 12-minute slog becomes a valuable piece of the whole.

Every mile matters; go run some.

November 24 - I will run outside!

Yep, it's Winter, the real deal. Between the weather and the busy holiday season coming up, it takes serious commitment to get out that door. Repeat after me, "I can run outside consistently this Winter, I will run outside consistently!" Okay, we are committed! This is not to say you will not put in a few treadmill miles if that's part of your jam, but that you will get out that door at least twice a week. One of the fulfilling aspects of the run is that it gets us outside. Our run gives us a chance to escape from our man-made caves and away from the air that we re-breathe with each other and to escape into the natural wonderful world. The treadmill won't give us a run into the sunrise with the light crunch of snow underfoot as a deer runs by, or a run that slaps us awake and lets us know we are truly alive, so, commit to run outside!

We will run outside, today!

November 25 - Run and give thanks

We are blessed to be runners and blessed by the rich race traditions of our sport. I'm a huge fan of Thanksgiving Day, a time to count our many blessings, a day to run, then get together with friends and family, and a time to use the words "thank you" a lot. It's also the day when more Americans enter races than any other day of the year, such as the proverbial Turkey Trots. Not all our days will be diamonds and we will all face dark days, but Thanksgiving reminds us to appreciate what we have and to find ways to bring some light to the darkness others are facing.

Run and give thanks.

November 26 - Rain and snow, go away, but I don't care either way

Never, ever, ever hesitate when it comes to the weather. Instead, get excited about the elements and the challenge before you. On Sunday morning I awoke to a single-digit day that had me stalling for a few more degrees before heading out. Finally out the door, I was greeted by a brilliant sunny day and light winds and was soon warm, in rhythm, enjoying every step and thinking, "I should have done this sooner and saved the mental energy!"

Get out there and put flight in the good fight.

November 27 - Hold on to what you have

As the Fall race season draws to an end, you might find the motivation to get out the door also coming to an end. Don't let this happen! Think of the shape you want to be in when it's time to line up again next Spring. Think of the personal records and goals you thought about during this running year and where you hope to be next year. CHAMPIONS ARE MADE IN WINTER! Take a couple of easy months away from high mileage and hard runs, but put in consistent Winter miles so you have the base needed to rock as the Spring run season heats up. Those who don't get the Winter miles in have to put up with the setbacks often seen while increasing mileage and getting "back" in shape. You will be starting out in Spring with a good mileage and strength base.

Use or lose it.

November 28 - Run and keep smiling!

The fitness lifestyle continues to grow in our culture, but so does the obesity rate. The U.S. adult obesity rate stands at 42.4 percent, the first time the national rate has passed the 40 percent mark, and further evidence of the country's obesity crisis. The national adult obesity rate has increased by 26 percent since 2008.(National Center for Health Statistics Data Brief

No. 360, February 2020, CDC.gov) So, as we head out for our run, we are perceived by many to be an oddball minority, those who choose to run and associate it with fun. All my running life I've heard the same comments, like, "I only run to the fridge or when I'm being shot at." When asked about my running, I find myself dumbing down my answers about how far I run or the races I enter. My hope is to make our sport less intimidating and more attainable. Yes, some of our athletic accomplishments might inspire others but I think what will help most is for more and more of us to get out there and set the example. When they see we are all shapes and sizes, running and walking, fast and slow, they may eventually get out to join us to find out what is so fun about the run.

Get out there, your run can change the world.

November 29 - The birthday run

Chances are, today is not your birthday. So may I suggest you make a note on the page of your birthdate to look here! If you have not already, today is the day to start a tradition that can motivate your running for the rest of your life. Run your age in miles, minutes, km's or something else you dream up. Your age is wonderfully personal, a number that you need to get your head around. A running tradition with your age is powerful. Start one! My first ultra was on my 50K birthday. Another tip--run your age up to 50, then subtract, instead of adding each year going forward, and at 100, you only need to get in one mile, minute, km or whatever.

You own today, go get it.

November 30 - Everything in moderation, including moderation!

Life is not meant to be lived in moderation. With a middle of the road life comes a middle of the road existence. Stress is in the eyes of the stressed. What could be more stressful than to look back at the years and wonder, what could I have done? Peace comes to those that already know that answer; they've done it! I believe life is meant to be lived out toward the edge. The proverbial edge is a personal point that is arrived at by means of your comfort zone. For some it might be an hour hike alone on trails in a state park, for others it might be a solo climb of a 20,000+ foot peak in the Himalayas. To us, I believe running gives us unlimited opportunities to get to the edge.

Go grab it.

December

December 1 - I love Winter, sure . . .

Let's face it, it's Winter. What's important is to get out the door. I'm not talking about every day or lots of miles, just about getting out the door on a regular basis to keep the fire lit. One of the reasons we run is its simplicity, requiring hardly anything. Yes, in Winter you need a few more layers, but in the grand scheme of Winter sports, running is still as basic as it gets. Winter brings darkness, icy winds, bad footing and most importantly, runs that give us the greatest feeling of accomplishment ever! We love Winter . . . .

Get out there.

December 2 - Tis the season, the hardest season to run

This time of year is like no other, the daily run is under constant assault from parties, family gatherings, work, to-do lists, crappy weather and short days. It will take a planned counterattack to hold your ground and get (squeeze) the run in. Have an extra set of running gear in your car and under your desk, and be prepared to shoot out the door whenever an opening strikes. Pull over while stuck in traffic, pull on the stuff and get in some miles. If an appointment gets canceled, get in a run before anyone has time to grab your hour. Forget about taking showers and primp time, forget about waiting to get home to a better run route; remember, those who are picky go without! Long blocks of time are at a premium; go for shorter and faster runs to satisfy the need for fatigue! Keep the faith, it won't be easy but nothing good ever is. We know that after a run, we are more productive and attentive workers and family members. At the next holiday gathering, you'll know you have won the war when you are the one who is relaxed, refreshed, smiling and patient in the frantic, party crowd, showing no wounds, and they will wonder how you did it!

The goal is noble not selfish, run.

December 3 - Chill out

On the first cold days of Winter you will find it easier to get out the door if you over-dress a bit. Start with a short loop where you can drop a layer once you feel out the weather. After the loop, continue your Winter runs into the wind--not fun--but knowing that at any time you can turn your back to the weather and have a more comfortable run home can provide the motivation to stick it out. Yes, many days we will just want to skip the Winter run . . . but as always, you will be happy that you ran, so don't think about it, just get out the door!

Run warm, run now.

December 4 - Run, recharge, share

The holidays are a time to get together with family and friends, to share and give of yourself. That said, don't forget to put aside one hour of each day for you, your health and wellbeing; an hour when you are not responsible for anyone else--work, family or friends— just your own mental and physical needs. Playtime! A time to fire up the senses, recharge the batteries and escape the digital 24/7, 365 rat race. Selfish? Not at all. Without taking this hour you will be as useless as a dead cell phone or a car out of gas on the shoulder of the road. Time to yourself will fill you with energy, creativity, contentment and joy, enough so that you'll have plenty to share!

Escape, now!

December 5 - Winter runs turn lies into truths

I admit, I used to whine a lot about cold Winter runs until I switched to lying and saying, "I love Winter." (Yes, I repeat the important stuff that works!) I found what they say is true, if you tell a lie long enough, you start to believe it. Try these lines: *I love the feel of the crunch of a new snow under my feet, the invigorating feel of a blast of cold crisp Winter air, the smug feeling of satisfaction I get from dressing well and taking command of my environment, and the impressive pile of fitness laundry I produce, proving I'm a serious athlete!* Yes, perhaps a stretch, but lies only work when there is a bit of truth to them. Whining will get you nowhere, lying will get you out the door and when you finish, amazingly, your lies will become the truth!

Lie, run, believe.

December 6 - Hello, have you accepted running as one of life's true gifts?

Some days I feel like I push running like the "Fuller Brush Christians" handing out their religious pamphlets door to door. Believe it or not, there are still people out there who don't run! Seriously though, I am thankful I have found running and what it has done for my life, so it's only natural to want to share this with others. May today's run leave you with peace, energy and a smile.

Run, amen.

December 7 – Your passion will guide you to a more perfect life

The passionate runner is a healthy eater. A high fat meal can't be followed by a run. The runner finds what to eat and when to eat to allow for the run. Don't worry about diet, become a runner and it will take care of itself. Insomnia issues, not to worry, the passionate runner will sleep soundly. Want to quit smoking? Become a passionate runner and smoking just goes away because it hampers your progress. The passion for a sport is a personal trainer, it motivates us out the door, every day, rain or shine.

Your passion will lead you . . . out the door

December 8 - I will not be feeling smart and happy today

As you know, I keep going back to the theme of the lack of motivation to get out the door and always coming back from the run smiling and happy we got out. Today, I face the opposite dilemma. I really feel like getting out there, but I have a bit of an Achilles pain and know I should take a couple of days off, dang. The worst part is that taking the day off will not leave me smiling and happy about it. Nothing about our sport is easy, nothing good comes easy. Running must be great because taking today off sucks! Because of today's difficult decision, most likely I'll be back out there pain-free in a few days feeling smart and smiling, before and after the run. Luckily, I'm PATIENT, damn it.

Run if you should.

December 9 - We are as tough as our runs

Yesterday as I headed onto the trails in a freezing drizzle after deciding to run hard and short to stay warm rather than the longer miles I planned on getting in, I was again struck by how hard our sport really is. We are not the proverbial average Americans; we are tough as nails dedicated athletes. Sure, we do it at different levels of discipline, but even getting out a couple of days a week for a few miles is hard work, work we choose to take on. Running is as difficult as sports get. We continue to fight the good fight because we know that at the end of every run, we are glad we did it and it is always worth it. Our brutal sport gives us back far more than we put into it, every time. Our run not only improves our mental and physical health, but prepares us to take on the adversities of a complicated world. Ya gotta love it!

Run into this crap, head on.

December 10 - It is so true, nothing good comes easy

We are reminded every time we layer up for our Winter runs that there is so much stuff to wear compared to a warm run and so much thought needed to decide what to wear, not to mention the increased laundry. All that said, after these runs, the amazing feeling of satisfaction and control of our lives that we get from them can't be explained or measured by the effort. A run that still gives back much more than all the work we put into it, more memorable and valuable than any fair-weather run will ever be. Dig it!

The run is always worth the effort.

December 11 - The season of giving

Those of us who are passionate runners know that running is truly a gift. Not only does the run add to our mental and physical health, but our quality of life, our self-esteem and so much more. Life without running would be quite different. Tis the season of giving. As with all that is good in life, we tend to want to share our experiences with others. Unfortunately, our passion for running can't be transferred. The passion must be found by the individual, but we can play a part. Yes, we can model our happiness and health and invite the beginning or potential runner along for a non-intimidating walk/run, but we all know toys are the best motivation to get people out the door. Consider giving motivational gifts your friends and family might want to try out, like running jacket, shoes or perhaps a GPS watch. Help light a flame that will burn forever, a true gift!

Buy running toys!

December 12 - Realistic resolutions

It's still a few weeks off, but NOW is the time to commit to some New Year's resolutions. Yes, people fail at resolutions all the time but then again, many make changes that stick. I'm a believer in realistic tweaks, working to be a better version of ourselves. As for running, perhaps start a new streak like committing to never run less than 3 days a week. This would be a good resolution for the runner who already runs 3 to 4 days but blows off a week now and then without an acceptable excuse. (There are no acceptable excuses!) After, let's say 6 months of not missing 3 days, one week starts badly and you have 3 days left and will need to run on all 3 days. The streak you have going will be powerful motivation to make it happen. Getting the 3 runs in will raise your self-esteem and motivate you to get in your runs early so this does not happen again. Picture this streak going on for 3 years and imagine the power of it! Consider small tweaks in other areas of life like your charitable giving, reductions in bad habits, and thoughtfulness to friends or skills you have wanted to learn but have procrastinated. Not trying is the only failure. Give it some thought on today's run, decide on a realistic goal and . . .

Commit!

December 13 - You are an athlete, you are a runner

If being an athlete sounds intimidating, you may have a different definition of "athlete" than mine. You become an athlete when you strive to get better at a sport in an organized manor. Gathering information, setting goals, competing and tracking your progress makes you an athlete. Age is irrelevant to this equation. You can become an athlete when you are 90 years old. May you continue your athletic pursuit, your personal journey. Yes, you are an athlete.

Now, get out there and prove it.

December 14 - To run your best, drink beer

This was the headline of an article I once read just after Frank Shorter won Olympic gold in Munich in 1972. It went on to explain that the two pints of beer Frank drank before the race was the reason he won the Olympic marathon. The facts: Alcohol is a diuretic that can lead to pre-race dehydration. Alcohol is also a depressant with many attributes that could seriously hurt athletic performance. For many runners, even one pint can cause stomach upset and other problems the morning after. Did the two pints help Frank Shorter win the gold? I believe the answer is yes. The drinks may have allowed him to fall asleep, avoiding the sleepless night that often comes before a major competition.

In the book by John Parker, *The Frank Shorter Story,* (published by *Runner's World Magazine*, 1972) John interviewed Frank and he admitted his fondness for beer, and how he got quite drunk the night before winning his Olympic gold medal in Munich. "That night we went out and I had a litre and a half or two of beer before bed. I didn't have any trouble sleeping at all. The German beer is great, and I really don't mind getting half-looped the night before a race."

I'm sure the many 100-mile weeks of running helped, along with some genetics. It also comes down to confidence in the things that you choose to do when training. Does this mean it is all mental and not physical? Not at all. When you have confidence in the actions you choose to take, you will take them very seriously and learn what is right for you. Besides, if you normally drink a beer each night, you should not do anything new the night before a race!

Cheers to today's run.

December 15 - Annual epic run

I write this today from Sedona, Arizona where I am about to embark on this year's epic run. Either solo or with a training partner, planning for an annual amazing run will add richness to your life. Ideally, come up with something just outside your comfort zone. In the planning, consider distance, elevation, destination, weather conditions and any aspect that will keep you excited and training. Personally, I plan an annual long trail run either solo or with my wife. This year it is 3 days in a row of long trail sections we mapped out. Technology has added a layer of safety and confidence to the epic run. By downloading a route in a phone app like Avenza, even without cell service, you can see where you are on the map.

Dream big on your run today,

December 16 - Short run absolution

As far as daylight hours, the next week or so will be the hardest to deal with, giving us about 8 measly hours of light. The Winter Solstice is soon, but the reality is the sun will stall for a few weeks on either side of the solstice before we inch into the longer days. Even as an obsessed runner, I believe the short days give us absolution for short runs! In two months, say mid-February, we'll have about an hour and a half more light than today. I'd say 20 percent more light deserves a 20 percent increase in weekly mileage, I'll up that another 25 percent by March 15th as the sun starts to do its job! A lot of BS? Perhaps, but an excuse for a plan nonetheless! That said, I just looked into why the daily average temperature drops after the shortest day of the year and the start of Winter, something that seemed to make no sense to me. It seems the earth's thermal mass takes a while to cool down after Summer. I'll be darned, and cold. Run short, sweet and perhaps in the dark, but . . .

Get out there and run!

December 17 - Run THROUGH it (Written by daughter Anna)

To the tune of *We're Going on a Bear Hunt:*

> We're going on a Winter run!
>
> We're gonna log some big miles!
>
> What a beautiful day!
>
> We're not scared.
>
> Uh oh! SNOW!
>
> Deep, slushy snow!
>
> We can't go over it.
>
> We can't go under it.
>
> WE'VE GOT TO GO THROUGH IT!

With a little preparation, a snowy run is the perfect addition to your training. Think of it as a totally unexpected bonus! Layer up your moisture-wicking clothing, throw on some traction devices and get your butt out the door. The varied footing of snowy miles works your ancillary muscles and connective tissues to enhance your balance and stability, making you SUPER STRONG; stuff you can't get on a treadmill! When the Spring run season hits you'll be totally prepared and you'll get to skip that getting "back" in shape phase!

We've got to go through it.

December 18 - Winding down

The weather suck sucks, but who cares. The racing season is behind us and for the most part, there are no scheduled miles to worry about. It's a time for short runs, days off, and perhaps a long run if we feel like it every other week or so, but not too long. We all need an off season, a time to ease up the miles and lick our wounds. That said, to make good use of the extra time we will have, might I suggest working on core strength and flexibility, something that many of us (me) neglect during the intense running months. It's time for some non-aerobic stuff, as I always say . . . dang

Run easy, but run.

December 19 - When it's pure hell out there

December in Michigan can bring snowy, gusty winds cracking in the trees, pinning our clothes to the body and taking our breath away, what I call a Rambo Run. December is no time to take your running seriously, just get out the door and keep some consistency. Forget long or fast, think, "Just get it in" and take pride in the fact that you are not a wimp! Just get out the door and be happy and proud with . . .

. . . whatever.

December 20 - The holiday screws are tightening

With gifts to buy, parties, dinners and visitors, in addition to the normal job and family requirements, getting in the daily run feels like lying, cheating and stealing--that is, until you get out the door! Once into the rhythm of the run, breathing in the cold fresh air and breaking into an honest sweat with your senses alive and the smoke clearing from your mind, finally comes the realization that this run was worth the cost!

Eat, drink, run and be merry, in any order necessary.

December 21 – Pain is your coach, it is not an injury

Running has taken a bad rap as an injury-prone sport. I cringe when I read articles badmouthing my sport. It must be true that bad news sells, reality be damned. I believe a part of the "running is bad for you" problem comes from runners who head to a doctor when they get a pain. For too many runners, especially new runners, the excitement and passion for the sport has them visiting a doctor in hopes of not missing a few days of running. A knee pain that could have been corrected by a more stable shoe, an arch support or a few days off is not what I would consider an injury, it's just the learning curve. Before you run to the doctor, take a week off, read all you can on the pain and its prevention with the extra time you have. Your knowledge will enrich your running life and help clear the misconceptions of our sport.

Run, recover and learn.

December 22 - This sport continues to amaze me

The physical and mental differences in people has made me accept the reality that training is more an art than a science. I have also determined that a successful outcome of training can be very different for different people. The training and goals must be adjusted to the individual's body, mind and sense of priority. A determined under-trained runner has a much better chance of making it to the finish line than a well-trained runner with doubts. A person who makes it to the starting line with family, friends and priorities intact may be well ahead (spiritually, mentally and physically) of his over-trained counterpart who ran on regardless of others. You will prevail if you understand that no other outcome is acceptable!

Train, believe, succeed.

December 23 - This is what we do for fun!

This is the thought that pops into my head whenever I'm in the pain zone. In training, this is what I ran this far to feel, the part where I come out the other side stronger, moving my needle, allowing me to run farther or faster the next time out. When racing, the pain hits and reminds me that I am not short-changing myself, that I've gone to the limit to see where I stand. Then I can judge myself and whatever the outcome--fast, slow, or wherever the chips land—know that I was heroic. Yes, only heroic to me, no one else could possibly know. It's as personal as it gets. Today I read that a two-time winner of the London Marathon and previous world record holder was charged with doping. Obviously I don't get it and perhaps am fortunate at some level not to get it. If I cheated, it would blow all I have achieved personally; it would be me failing myself. It would be anything but fun.

If it's not fun, don't do it. But you know better!

December 24 - I love the marathon distance

Unlike a shorter race where I'm sure I will finish, although not sure if my time will end up according to plan, the marathon is like sailing out into the ocean at an approaching storm. I know I will be tossed and tested, I know there will be hell to pay, but I also know that when it hits, I will break out in a smile knowing this is exactly what I came for. In a recent marathon, just past mile 21, my world got dark. I laughed, smiled, shed a tear and took inventory. I changed my form, searching for unused muscles that might have a bit of glycogen left. I made goals of not walking until the next mile mark, until the next block, until the next crack in the road. I imagined I was being lifted and pushed forward by an imaginary force; I yelled out like a madman, "It's time to pick up the pace and take it home!" and for a few yards, I actually did, so I tried this again, nope. I fought pain, I lost coordination, I stumbled but did not fall, and after an eternity of struggle, the darkness cleared and I could just make out the sign--mile 26. New Year's resolution time is here. You don't have to run a marathon to enjoy this running life, just sayin'.

Take it to the limit.

December 25 - Oh, the weather outside is frightful

But you might as well trick the family out for a walk around the block! Bundle them up and the gang will be laughing all the way! Be the catalyst for some fit and fun fresh air. Be subtle at first, then talk the adventure up like it's Shackleton's expedition to the Pole and worth breaking away from the TV! We live in a Winter wonderland, why not start a Christmas Day, fresh air tradition that includes going toe to toe and getting slapped around by Mother Nature, and when you dash back inside, the fire will be so much more delightful!

Run, run, Rudolph.

December 26 - The pain was perfect

These guys were the regulars, I was the guest. First came a quick explanation of the 5.2-mile route, a Winter route designed to follow streetlights, not quite enough light, but as good as it gets on the far edge of suburbia. We headed into the night. Only about 200 yards into it and the pace was heating up. No conversation. I had the feeling that I was as strong as any in the group, at least the ones who counted, those I knew. Cool. About a half-mile of this and we settled in; I liked what I felt. We were quickly down to a lead pack of 5 from the original 12. Everyone I expected was there, including a couple I knew would soon be in a world of hurt. I respect that; I'm there often. I broke the silence to feel them out. I was making comments more than asking questions but the quiet was telling. A few long hilly miles, but we seemed to be hitting a nice groove. Finally, a long downhill--my strength, two guys pushed it up. I went along, they pushed it more. The pain was perfect. I was working big-time and could sense I wasn't alone. No one backed down. Just as the world started to fog over, another turn and we were at the finish! We jogged an easy recovery mile talking, joking and celebrating the effort. The wind picked up and the night turned cold--or was it this way all the time? We had been lost for a while in the magic world of speed and effort. Night speed, it gets no better.

Get lost in your run, enjoy.

December 27 - Why not double dip?

We head out and run for play, for escape and for personal time but it's so much more than that. In addition to the pure joy of running, we are logging miles, we are increasing our fitness level and perhaps chipping away at our long-term running goals. We are not just having fun, although that alone is perhaps good enough reason for what we do. We are in training, we are athletes, we are getting better at it. Running and training lets us double-dip some of the best things in this running life. Heck, why would we ever not run when the chance is before us?

If you have the day off, perhaps run twice today!

December 28 - A time for totals

As we log the final miles of the running year, I'm reminded of the tremendous motivational value of the log. You may no longer be able to set a PR at a race, but streaks and total mileage PRs are always out there. Totals--like the most mileage ran in a day, a week, or a year. Streaks--like the most days ran in a row or some other motivational streak like number of weeks in a row that you ran at least 3 days. December is a month we need extra motivation to sneak in those runs. If you only need a few miles to hit an annual goal of say, 500 miles, the log will get you out that door. If you don't keep a log, I suggest you add it to your resolutions!

Run and write it down.

December 29 - We are a work in progress

I've had some success over the years with New Year's resolutions. I'm sure we can all think of 50 bad behaviors we'd like to change, but I find if you get it down to one or two that seem like they have realistic possibilities for success, we have a good shot at tweaking this life for the better. Let's make a commitment to ourselves and have the courage to start. Yes, we can change. A big one for me was giving up my daily Pepsi or Coke. I've been soft drink-free for 12 years. Yes, these changes can stick. The trick is to get the streak going. The longer the streak, the more it will drive us to success.

Be a better you, start with today's run.

December 30 - Don't let injury stop you from your resolutions

For those of you starting off the year with an injury that is keeping you from your run, your goal is set for you! Continue to research and set a course of action to get healthy and back on track. Training or recovering--it's all part of the journey. Take satisfaction in your commitment, no matter how slow the progress, or even in case of a setback, you are on a mission of self-discovery! Hang tough!

Enjoy the adventure, on or off the road to personal fulfillment.

December 31 - res·o·lu·tion: A resolve; a decision or determination: *to make a firm resolution to do something*

There is a lot of joking this time of year about failed New Year's resolutions, but for us who run and walk on a regular basis, it's no joke. We speak with our feet and do what we plan. So yes, we don't fit the average American mold; we know from experience what it takes to reach goals and make positive changes in our lives. We know the value of the hard work we are about to do and that the success of our long-term goals are worth the effort--physically, mentally and personally. I'll see you out on the roads and trails as we log our miles, set personal bests and keep our streaks going!

Get out and prove them wrong, today, tomorrow, forever.

I hope you found value in this book

As we let the participants in our events know in our post-race emails, it is not lost on us that with thousands of events out there to choose from, you took the gamble and put faith in ours with your hard earned entry money and even more so, that you trusted the time and effort of your training, and our thanks goes deep.

The same sentiment is what I'm trying to share regarding my book. There are millions to choose from out there and you took a chance on mine. I can only hope that you found it insightful and motivational and if so, please share your valuable opinion with the running world and give it a review. It would mean a lot to me if you let me personally know your thoughts, positive or negative. Your input will help me shape future editions and will be helping fellow running reader. Email randy@rfevents.com. Check out the calendar of events at rfevents.com, and I hope to see you line up with us some day!

Now, put down the book and get out that door!

Acknowledgements

This book was made possible by the crew at RF Events, who encouraged me and gave me the okay to take the time to write it. Big-time thanks to my daughter, kid, Anna "Baby Goat," who wrote a few incredibly motivational entries that are peppered throughout the book. I also want to thank my partner Steve for putting up with me and the hundreds of dedicated staff members who have worked at Running Fit and RF Events over the years, sharing their knowledge and love of our sport and encouraging thousands to get out the door and run. Thanks to my kind, loving, caring, smart wife and life-long running partner Kathy, for making me a better person.

Made in the USA
Monee, IL
27 January 2021

58863239R00134